DEVIL'S ADVOCATES

DEVIL'S ADVOCATES is a series of books devoted to exploring the classics of horror cinema. Contributors to the series come from the fields of teaching, academia, journalism and fiction, but all have one thing in common: a passion for the horror film and a desire to share it with the widest possible audience.

'The admirable Devil's Advocates series is not only essential – and fun – reading for the serious horror fan but should be set texts on any genre course.'
Dr Ian Hunter, Reader in Film Studies, De Montfort University, Leicester

'Auteur Publishing's new Devil's Advocates critiques on individual titles... offer bracingly fresh perspectives from passionate writers. The series will perfectly complement the BFI archive volumes.' **Christopher Fowler,** *Independent on Sunday*

'Devil's Advocates has proven itself more than capable of producing impassioned, intelligent analyses of genre cinema... quickly becoming the go-to guys for intelligent, easily digestible film criticism.' *Horror Talk.com*

'Auteur Publishing continue the good work of giving serious critical attention to significant horror films.' *Black Static*

 DevilsAdvocatesbooks

 DevilsAdBooks

LET THE RIGHT ONE IN

DEVIL'S ADVOCATES

ANNE BILLSON

auteur

First published in 2011, reprinted 2014 by
Auteur, 24 Hartwell Crescent, Leighton Buzzard LU7 1NP
www.auteur.co.uk
Copyright © Auteur 2011

Series design: Nikki Hamlett at Cassels Design
Set by Cassels Design www.casselsdesign.co.uk
Printed and bound by CPI Group (UK) Ltd, Croydon, CR0 4YY

Images from *Let the Right One In* taken from the Momentum Region 2 DVD © Bavaria Media GmbH; *Frostbiten* taken from the Soda Pictures Region 2 DVD © Fido Film AB; *Dracula* © Universal Pictures; *Dracula* © Hammer Film Productions; *Bram Stoker's Dracula* © Columbia Pictures; *Martin* © Laurel Entertainment; *Near Dark* © F/M; *The Hunger* © MGM; *Interview with the Vampire* © Geffen Pictures; *Buffy the Vampire Slayer* © 20th Century Fox Television; *Twilight* © Summit Entertainment; *Daughters of Darkness* © Showking Films

British Library Cataloguing-in-Publication Data
A catalogue record for this book is available from the British Library

ISBN: 978-1-906733-50-6
ISBN: 978-1-906733-96-4 (e-book)

CONTENTS

INTRODUCTION

Vampires have never been so popular. *Twilight, True Blood, Being Human, The Vampire Diaries,* the novels of Anne Rice and Darren Shan, *Buffy the Vampire Slayer,* the *Blade* and *Underworld* series have all combined to create a new generation which can't get enough of these bloodsuckers. Amid this glut of vampire fiction it takes a very special vampire movie to stand out from the crowd.

This is a book about the Swedish vampire film, *Låt den rätte komma in,* which not only stands out from contemporary vampire films, but ranks among the very best vampire movies of the past century. It was directed by Tomas Alfredson and written for the screen by John Ajvide Lindqvist, who adapted it from his own novel of the same name. Lindqvist's inspiration for the title of his novel was 'Let the Right One Slip In', a song by the lugubrious British rock singer-songwriter Morrissey, formerly of the band The Smiths.

> And when at last it does
> I'd say you were within your rights to bite
> The right one and say, 'What kept you so long?'

For the purposes of this book, I shall be using the English title *Let the Right One In* throughout the text, and all quotations from the dialogue will be taken from the English subtitles. Unless otherwise indicated all quotations by Alfredson and Lindqvist are taken from the DVD commentary (Momentum Pictures, 2009). To avoid confusion, the character of Eli, introduced as a girl though of ambiguous gender in both the novel and (to a lesser extent) the film, will be referred to throughout the text with the pronouns 'she' and 'her'.

Let the Right One In had its world premiere on 26 January 2008 at the Göteborg International Film Festival in Sweden and was screened at other festivals in Europe, North America, Australia and South Korea. It went on general release in Sweden and Norway in October 2008, before being released in other territories, including the US in October 2008, France in February 2009 and the United Kingdom in April 2009. Since this book was begun, an American remake with the title *Let Me In* (2010) has appeared, directed by Matt Reeves, previously best known for the monster movie *Cloverfield* (2008).

In English-speaking territories the title was translated as *Let the Right One In*, and in most European languages the title was a variation on the phrase, 'Let Me In', with the notable exceptions of German (where it was called *So finster die Nacht* - 'So Dark the Night') and French (where it was called *Morse* - presumably a reference to the Morse Code by which the two main characters communicate with each other, but also perhaps hinting at the word 'morsure', French for 'bite'). Other variations include the Argentine title, *Criatura de la noche* ('Creature of the Night').

In the following text, I will attempt to explain why *Let the Right One In* not only stands out from other recent vampire films, but also stands head and shoulders above other recent horror movies. Like *Twilight* (2008), it's a love story between a human and a vampire, but there the resemblance ends; *Let the Right One In* has fantastical elements, but is emphatically not a romantic fantasy. It's set in the real world, and pulls off the seemingly impossible trick of combining two apparently incompatible genres: the vampire movie and the social realist drama.

But while the film is startlingly original, it could scarcely have existed without the 86 years of vampire cinema that preceded it. So I'm not only going to examine how the film's approach, mood and technique set it apart from other vampire and horror movies; I'm also going to look at how it has drawn from, and spun intriguing new twists on, classic vampire films, at how vampire cinema has already flirted with social realism, and at how vampire mythology adapts itself to the modern world. I shall also examine the nature of the relationship between vampire and human, the role of the vampire's assistant and the reasons why the vampire has become such an enduring and iconic figure in today's popular culture.

SYNOPSIS

The year is 1981. The action takes place over an approximately two week period in Blackeberg, a working-class suburb to the west of Stockholm, Sweden, where 12-year-old Oskar lives in a small flat with his divorced mother. He's a solitary, delicate-looking child who collects press cuttings about murders, plays with a knife and entertains violent fantasies about getting his own back on the classmates who bully him at school. In the yard in front of the block of flats, he meets Eli, a girl of around his age who has just moved in next door to Oskar with Håkan, a middle-aged man posing as her father.

Oskar doesn't know it yet, but Eli needs to drink blood to survive. In nearby Vällingby, Håkan murders a youth in the park, but is interrupted before he has finished collecting his victim's blood, which he then leaves behind in his panic. Driven by thirst, Eli attacks a local man, Jocke, and drinks his blood before killing him. Unknown to her, a man called Gösta, who lives with his cats, sees the murder from a window overlooking the scene. Håkan disposes of Jocke's corpse in a nearby icy lake.

Oskar lends Eli a Rubik's Cube puzzle, which she solves overnight; he teaches himself Morse code and shares his new-found knowledge with Eli, so they can communicate with each other by tapping on the party wall between their flats.

After school, the bullies torment Oskar, leaving him with a cut on his cheek; he lies to his mother about the wound, telling her he fell down, but shares the truth with Eli, who advises him to fight back. Oskar begins to attend weight-training and swimming classes in an attempt to build up his strength. Håkan, increasingly unhappy about Eli's friendship with the boy next door, botches another attempt to collect blood from a victim, and pours acid over his own face in a despairing effort to hide his identity. Horribly disfigured and unable to speak, he is arrested and taken to hospital. Eli tracks him down, and scales the hospital wall up to the window of his room, where he offers his own blood to her before falling to his death.

Eli sneaks into Oskar's bedroom, and they chastely sleep together in his bed. She agrees to be his girlfriend, but returns to her apartment before dawn, leaving him a note: 'I must go and live, or stay and die. ♥ Yours, Eli.' ('I must be gone and live, or stay and die.' - Romeo and Juliet) On a school skating trip to the lake, Conny, ringleader of the bullies, threatens to dunk Oskar in the icy water; Oskar follows Eli's advice and strikes back with a rod he's picked up, leaving Conny deaf in one ear. At the same time, two small girls start screaming; they've spotted Jocke's corpse frozen in the ice.

Oskar leads Eli into a utility area of the swimming pool used by local youngsters as a den and deliberately cuts his hand, wanting to exchange his blood with her as a sign of friendship. Eli backs away at the sight of the blood, but can't resist dipping down to lap it up from the floor. She orders Oskar to leave.

Her appetite whetted, Eli attacks and bites Virginia, who has just had an argument with her boyfriend Lacke, but Lacke arrives on the scene before Eli can deal the death blow. The next day, Virginia finds she can no longer tolerate daylight, which burns her skin, and feels an overwhelming urge to drink blood. On a visit to Gösta's flat she is attacked by his cats and falls down the stairs. Lacke accompanies her to hospital. Realising Eli's bite has somehow infected her and not wanting to live, she asks a nurse to open the blinds of her room and bursts into flame. Lacke arrives on the scene just in time to see her burning up.

Oskar goes to stay with his father in the countryside, where he enjoys himself until a neighbour turns up, and the two men start drinking. Oskar runs away and hitches a lift back to Stockholm. He calls on Eli and asks her directly if she is a vampire. Eli admits she has been 12-years-old for a very long time and shows Oskar that, despite the bareness of her flat, she is not short of money. He accuses her of having stolen it from her victims and leaves. Later, she rings his doorbell and explains that he must invite her in. He refuses, so she enters without an invitation and starts to bleed all over. In a panic, Oskar relents and issues the invitation. Later, when Eli is changing into clean clothes, Oskar glimpses a scar on her pubic area.

Lacke, determined to avenge Virginia and his dead friend Jocke, tracks Eli to the bathroom where she sleeps during the day; Oskar, who has been sleeping under the table in Eli's flat, distracts Lacke before he can do her harm, and backs away from the bathroom as Eli kills him. The sounds of the murder disturb the neighbours, and Eli realises she has to leave. Oskar watches from his window as a taxi takes her away.

Oskar gets a phone call from Martin, one of the bullies, who pretends to be friendly but is luring Oskar into a trap. Oskar is subsequently cornered at the swimming-pool by the bullies. Jimmy, Conny's older brother, threatens to blind him in one eye unless he can stay underwater for three minutes and forces Oskar's head down. Just as it looks as though Oskar might drown, Eli breaks into the building, kills the bullies and rescues Oskar.

Oskar is on a train; he appears to be alone in the carriage, but there is knocking from the large trunk on the floor beside him. Oskar taps back the message 'kiss' in Morse code.

'BE ME, FOR A LITTLE WHILE'

Let the Right One In is one of the best new horror films since the genre's last great creative flourishing in the 1970s. But to describe the impact it had on me, I need to provide some back story, particularly for the benefit of readers who grew up watching the horror movies made in the 1990s or the 2000s, and who look on films such as *The Lost Boys* (1987) or *Bram Stoker's Dracula* (1993) or even *Blade* (1998) as venerable classics of vampire cinema.

I daresay there may even be readers whose entire knowledge of vampires has been gleaned from *Twilight*. *Let the Right One In*'s Eli is, as we shall see, a type of vampire very different to Edward Cullen, the undead hero of *Twilight*. But movie vampires go back a lot further than these two. They come in all shapes and styles, and the vampire myth is both durable and flexible enough to embrace many different permutations.

When I was small, vampires were not considered suitable subject matter for children and were confined to X-rated movies; no-one under the age of eighteen, or at least no-one who *looked* younger than 18-years-old, was allowed into the cinema to watch horror films. It would be another twenty years before video recorders became standard household equipment, so the only way of watching such films at home was when they were shown on television. Child-friendly vampires such as Count Duckula, Bunnicula, Count Chocula breakfast cereal, the Count on *Sesame Street* (1969–) and *The Little Vampire* (1979) by Angela Sommer-Bodenburg were still a long way off, and indeed were unthinkable in that era. Vampires were unequivocally evil; the 'good' or sympathetic vampire had yet to be invented, and the idea of making friends with a vampire, let alone falling in love with one, was inconceivable.

So I was 10 before I glimpsed my very first vampire. I saw him on television in an episode of *Doctor Who* called *Journey Into Terror* (1965), part four of a second season story called *The Chase*. The Doctor, who had yet to regenerate for the first time and was still being played as a grouchy old man by William Hartnell, and his companions (Ian, Barbara and Vicki) are chased through time and space by the Daleks, who pursue them from the top of the Empire State Building to the Marie Celeste (the crew and passengers abandon ship when they see the Daleks) and thence into what appears to be a haunted house, where they encounter a Grey Lady, Frankenstein's Monster and Count Dracula.

It wasn't until I took another look at this episode several decades later that I saw the house wasn't a real haunted house, as I'd remembered it, but a futuristic theme park attraction called 'The Festival of Ghana', that the future being referred to was 1996, and that the ghost and the monsters were in fact robots. But it didn't matter, because the way the Dracula robot stepped forward and said 'I am Count Dracula', in a sinister Slav accent, caught my imagination. Who was this person, and why was he so scary? I immediately loved the very name 'Dracula', probably because it was a cross between the word 'dragon' (in Romanian, the word 'dracul' can mean either 'dragon' or 'devil') and 'Graculus', the name of a large talking bird in Oliver Postgate's children's TV series *Noggin the Nog* (1959-65). Thus it evoked two of the things I loved reading about as a child: dragons, and Norse sagas. I hadn't a clue who Count Dracula was or what he did, but I was already hooked.

Though I was too small to sneak into cinemas to see X-rated films, I wasn't too young to be an avid reader of the film magazines which were given away free at any local cinema, and which often contained set reports and stills of forthcoming releases, including horror films. I was particularly intrigued by a Hammer movie called *The Kiss of the Vampire* (1963) and anything starring Christopher Lee, who both frightened and fascinated me.

Ironically, by the time I was old enough to see vampire movies in the cinema, the subgenre was in decline. Hammer's aristocratic bloodsuckers and their bosomy victims in elaborate period frocks (sometimes the female vampires were bosomy too) and the country house settings seemed quaint compared to the New Wave of horror ushered in by George Romero's flesh-eating zombies in *Night of the Living Dead* (1968), followed by the same director's social realist vampire movie *Martin* (1977) and David Cronenberg's early excursions into body-horror, *Shivers* (1975) and *Rabid* (1977), neither of which were vampire movies in the strictest sense, but which nevertheless seemed to be taking the idea of vampirism to another, even more horrific level.

Count Yorga, Vampire (1970) and *The Return of Count Yorga* (1971) transplanted a Dracula-type vampire into a modern urban setting, and I fainted at a late-night screening of the more traditional *Grave of the Vampire* (1974) at the Holloway Odeon (I recently discovered the screenplay had been written by David Chase, who would go on to create *The Sopranos* [1999-2007]) but that was due more to my own lurid imagination than to anything actually depicted on screen; a young woman, raped by a vampire, gives birth to a vampire baby which refuses to drink her milk but laps at her blood when she cuts her finger. I had a sudden horrible notion that she was going to slice off her nipple and offer the mutilated breast to her baby (which is when I passed out) but mercifully she didn't. Otherwise, traditional vampire films were off the agenda for most of the 1970s, though vampire fiction was not; everyone I knew read Stephen King's *Salem's Lot* (1975) and Anne Rice's *Interview with the Vampire* (1976). Rice's *Vampire Chronicles*, of which *Interview* was the first, did a lot to keep the vampire flame burning throughout what, in cinematic terms, were the relatively lean years of the late 1970s and 1980s, while movie vampires were largely played for laughs in spoofs such as *Love at First Bite* (1979), *Saturday the 14th* (1981) and *Once Bitten* (1985), the latter starring a young Jim Carrey.

Just as they appeared to have degenerated into terminal parody, vampires began to come back into fashion, spearheaded by the box-office success of the horror-comedies *Fright Night* (1985) and *The Lost Boys*, and *Bram Stoker's Dracula*, directed by Francis Coppola, who wasn't a genre director but a highly respected A-lister. But the factor which really brought vampires out of the horror ghetto and established them as leading players in the consciousness of a new generation was *Buffy the Vampire Slayer*, which made little impact in film form (1992) but when rebooted as a TV show (1997-2003), turned into a cultural phenomenon, its fame and popularity boosted by the rapidly expanding new medium of the internet, where fans would gather, in a virtual sense, to analyse and discuss details of each new episode in blogs and forums. Vampires, once confined to the horror genre, were no longer an interest peculiar to Goths, nerds or horror fans – they had invaded the mainstream.

Post-*Buffy*, vampires polarised into two kinds of movie, both apparently influenced by the TV show. On the one hand were CGI-heavy comic-strip action franchises like *Blade* and *Underworld* (2003) and their sequels, in which vampires dressed in tight black leather and bounced off the walls doing supernatural martial arts either against each other or against other creatures such as werewolves. On the other, the vampire protagonists of Anne Rice's *Vampire Chronicles* and Chelsea Quinn Yarbro's historical novels featuring the vampire Count St-Germain were being increasingly watered down into the heroes of a new strain of paranormal romantic fiction in which vampires took the place of Heathcliff or Mr Darcy in the romantic fantasies of young female readers, a trend culminating in the *Twilight* novels of Stephenie Meyer.

These new model vampires could often still be killed in traditional ways such as a stake through the heart or sunlight, but – fangs, bloodsucking and longevity apart – there didn't seem a lot to distinguish them from non-supernatural action heroes or villains. Both the romantic and the action-orientated stories featured heroic as well as villainous vampires, and both types caught the imagination of younger audiences. But neither type of vampire appealed much to me. I liked my vampires evil, or at least more dangerous to human health than *Twilight*'s Edward Cullen, or *Underworld*'s Selene.

Through the years, I have seen vampire fads come and go. I have seen vampires transformed from the ghastly walking cadavers of Carpathian myth into evil demons into vicious sexual predators into cuddly children's toys into broody romantic heroes and even role models. By the time my own vampire novel, *Suckers*, was published in 1993, vampire fans were already looking on vampires as creatures to be admired, as one can see from some of the comments on amazon.com, where readers complained that I 'didn't bring out the magnificence of the vampyres', and that I 'made vampire existence out to be shallow, carping and empty.'

I'd love to know what those readers thought about Eli in *Let the Right One In*.

The trailer looked promising. It was low-key, didn't give too much away, and appeared to be a refreshing change from *Blade* or *Underworld* or even *Buffy the Vampire Slayer*. There had already been hints on internet blogs and forums that this Swedish film about the friendship between a pre-pubescent boy and a young female vampire was something special. The film was screened to a rapturous reception at 2008's Frightfest in London, but since I was then living in France and was unable to attend I was forced to wait until it opened in Paris in February 2009. (Surprisingly, *Let the Right One In* attracted little critical attention in France, perhaps because the French title, *Morse*, wasn't very compelling; I have since encountered several discerning French cinephiles who had never even heard of it.)

When, at last, I was able to see the film for myself, I found it unusually tense and frightening, not so much because of the vampire, but because I was terrified of what the bullies might do to Oskar, and what might Lacke might do to Eli; I was in Oskar and Eli's corner from outset. The film and its characters both repelled and attracted me; they were neither glamorous nor heroic, nor were they people I would care to meet in real life, but I felt for them. I felt not just the loneliness of Oskar and Eli, but the disappointment of secondary characters such as Lacke and Virginia. I even felt sorry for the creepy paedophiliac Håkan. *Let the Right One In* wasn't just a horror film, it was a love story, but one of the strangest love stories I'd ever seen – sex didn't even enter into it – and one that raised troubling questions about the nature of love itself.

Let the Right One In, virtually single-handedly, restored my waning appetite for vampires and horror in general, demonstrating an exciting and original approach to vampire film conventions, and persuading me the genre was still rich in possibilities. It ignored contemporary horror film trends and gave me a taste of the old excitement from the 1970s, when local or repertory cinemas would be showing new horror films by David Cronenberg, Jeff Lieberman, George Romero, Tobe Hooper, Larry Cohen, Brian De Palma or Wes Craven, and, week after week, I would see things I'd never seen before: visions which amazed, disturbed or inspired me. The horror movies of the 1970s broke taboos, subverted conventions, tested the spectators' limits and stretched the definition of the genre in a way that has rarely been done, before or since.

Unusually for the modern horror genre, less rich in subtext than its 1970s equivalent, *Let the Right One In* is open to multiple interpretations and hints at something going on beneath the surface. Its characters are more than just good and evil cyphers. The story has you not just sympathising with but actively rooting for a serial killer, a potential serial killer, and an illicit partnership which will almost certainly result in the deaths of innocent parties in the very near future. It requires audiences to exercise their imaginations, which have the potential to be far more powerful and unsettling than any amount of explicit gore and shock-horror moments from all but the most talented and visionary film-makers. It's a film which sticks with you, which makes you think about it when it's over. And there's a lot to think about.

TEXTUAL ANALYSIS

ARE YOU A VAMPIRE?

GENRE

> I wanted to approach my subject completely seriously and absolutely reject all... sort of 'romanticized' notions about vampires, or what we've seen earlier of vampires, and just concentrate on the question: If a child was stuck forever like, in a 12-year-old existence and had to walk around killing other people and drink their blood to live – what would that child's existance really be like? If you disregard all the romanticized clichés. And then it struck me when I wrote the book that it would be an absolutely horrible existence. Miserable, gross and lonely. (John Ajvide Lindqvist, interview with 'The Northlander', Ain't It Cool News, 23 October 2008)

You can interpret *Let the Right One In* in any one of several ways. For example:

1. As a love story between two lonely pubescent children, one of whom happens to be a vampire.

2. As the story of a boy who befriends a serial killer.

3. As a story in which a centuries-old vampire 'grooms' a pubescent boy to replace the human helper who is growing old, ugly and inept.

4. As a story in which a solitary boy, bullied at school, conjures up a soulmate with supernatural powers who will help him fight back against the bullies.

Even before it was released, the film was already being acknowledged as a modern classic, and in a class of its own, distinct from other contemporary vampire and horror movies, and offering a new spin on an old genre. With remarkably few exceptions, the critical reception was overwhelmingly positive. Philip French in *The Observer* (12 April 2009) called it, 'a major addition to the vampire genre.' Manohla Dargis of *The New York Times* (24 October 2008) called in 'spectrally beautiful.' Kim Newman in *Empire* (9 April 2009) awarded it five stars and called it, 'a devastating, curiously uplifting inhuman drama and a superbly crafted genre exercise.'

But which genre, exactly? As Mark Kermode has pointed out (*Sight & Sound*, May 2009, p35), *Let the Right One In* 'falls into that category of truly great movies which are best defined not by what they are, but by what they are not'.

Eli is nothing like traditional movie vampires such as Dracula or Elizabeth Báthory, and the only thing she seems to have in common with more recent movie vampires, such as Selene from the *Underworld* films or Edward Cullen from the *Twilight* series, is her preternatural strength and speed. As in *Twilight* and the TV series *Buffy the Vampire Slayer* at least one of the protagonists in *Let the Right One In* is of school age; there are scenes set in the classroom, school corridors and grounds, and a pivotal scene takes place on a school field trip, but this is not a school story any more than a traditional horror or vampire film.

The film also offers several new twists on the old traditions and elements of coming-of-age stories, childhood fantasy and serial killer movies. And while its approach to the vampire myth is startlingly original, it does have its antecedents; *Let the Right One In* could not exist without the vampire movies and novels that preceded it. It both draws from and subverts the conventions and symbolism of classic vampire mythology, and adds a surprising element which has rarely been seen in vampire movies in the past, and which you absolutely do not associate with vampires – social realism, the definition of which is, 'a very broad term for painting (or literature or other art) that comments on contemporary social, political, or economic conditions, usually from a left-wing viewpoint, in a realistic manner' (The Concise Oxford Dictionary of Art and Artists, Ian Chilvers, 2003). Social realism thus appears to be completely at odds with the very notion of mythical creatures such as vampires. How can they possibly mix?

Though one of its two main characters is a vampire, *Let the Right One In* doesn't slot easily into the standard horror movie template, nor does it pander to any of the most common post-Millennium tendencies in fantasy cinema. It features blood-drinking, spontaneous combustion, spontaneous haemorrhage, mutilation and serial-killing, and ends with the massacre of children – all prime horror film ingredients.

But the film has little in common with the major horror film tendencies of the twenty-first century. For example, unlike *Saw* (2004), *Hostel* (2005) or *Martyrs* (2008), it contains no scenes of imprisonment or torture. Eli kills her victims quickly, and appears to take no pleasure at all in the act of murder. Her motivation for killing is purely as a means to survive; the unfortunate victim is collateral damage, and it's clearly not her intention to inflict distress, fear or pain. Virginia's sufferings are accidental, a result of Eli being interrupted before she can can finish what she has started. To extract the vital blood for his vampire 'mistress', Håkan uses no infernal instruments of torture, as in the *Saw* movies, or elaborate Heath Robinson-style death-traps, as featured in *Final Destination* (2000) and its sequels; his 'murder kit' is made up of of everyday household objects, which are neither fetishised nor treated with particular care. He doesn't even seem to keep them very clean.

EDITING

In contrast to the editing in a lot of contemporary movies, not just horror films, which seem to be cut for the benefit of audiences suffering from Attention Deficit Disorder, the editing by Alfredson and Dino Jonsäter is calm and measured, with many long, slow takes. There are none of the techniques once thought cutting edge, but which have now become visual clichés: jump-cuts, ultra-rapid cutting and cross-cutting, subliminal flashbacks and flashforwards, freeze frames, slo-mo and variable frame speeds which accelerate time or make characters move jerkily. This absence of gimmickry makes the editing seem stylistically appropriate to the early 1980s, the period in which the story is set; it might almost be a film from the early 1980s, and it avoids revelling in the sort of retro-date-stamping that would have made it an exercise in 1980s nostalgia. Whereas most modern horror films are fated by their style to seem dated after only a few years, *Let the Right One In* will almost certainly continue to look as elegant and timeless as it does today.

ACTION

Let the Right One In establishes a slow and steady rhythm right from the start, and although it contains violent action, it's devoid of the sort of scenes of combat featured in the *Blade* and *Underworld* films, which incorporate highly stylised, comic book-style martial arts and stuntwork. The swimming-pool massacre, which in a more conventional film would be the big action highlight and the perfect excuse for plenty of vampire-fu as Eli kicks ass and rips heads off, is not shown directly, but rather conveyed as a series of impressions from Oskar's point of view as he's held underwater.

There is no extended subjective tracking camerawork to represent the vampire stalking her victim. Eli doesn't leap into frame expressly to startle us; her attacks are sudden and she certainly startles her victims, but they're filmed in long or medium shot, putting distance between us and the violence and obliging us to consider it objectively rather than become viscerally or emotionally involved. She doesn't play with her food, doesn't take sadistic pleasure from killing and is not showing off. It's simply something she needs to do to survive.

FRAMING AND CAMERA MOVEMENT

Blackeberg: depressing ranks of identical square windows

There are none of the faux-documentary signifiers – natural lighting, hand-held video camera, seemingly unprofessional acting – characteristic of low budget horror since *The Blair Witch Project* (1999). Unlike *Paranormal Activity* (2007), the Spanish movie *[Rec]* (2007) and its American remake *Quarantine* (2008), *Let the Right One In* could not conceivably be mistaken for the work of amateurs. Alfredson uses the widescreen 2:35 format and Hoyte Van Hoytema's cinematography is as measured and precise as the editing, with each shot a small masterpiece of elegant framing and focus manipulation. Camera movement, when there is any, is limited to the occasional steady pan or tracking shot. The film-makers frequently exploit depth of field in the two-shots, focusing on one character while another is less sharp on another plane. They also give us compositions in which the frame is divided into more than one perfectly focused segment, each containing a different character and a different piece of action; Oskar's mother talking to Oskar from the kitchen, for example, while in the other part of the frame Oskar takes the newspaper from a table in the living room. Or Håkan slumped defeated in the shower room in one part of the frame, while on the other side the youth he has hung upside-down from the coathooks is being rescued by his friends.

SOUNDTRACK

The makers of horror films today often pepper their soundtracks with sudden loud bursts of music for no reason other than to try and make audiences jump. Or they use sinister or edgy music to try and build tension. Or they try and pump up the audience's adrenalin with aggressive rock music. By contrast, Johan Söderqvist's score for Let the Right One In is wistful and romantic, more the sort of music one associates with a love story or emotional drama than with a horror movie, and it's used sparingly. 'The music should emphasise the romantic parts of the film rather than the scary parts,' says Alfredson. There is precedent for this sort of counteractive scoring in horror movies such as Rosemary's Baby (1968) in which Christopher Komeda's lullaby suggests mother love over horror; or in Four Flies on Grey Velvet (1971), in which one of Ennio Morricone's loveliest, most lyrical themes accompanies a slow-motion decapitation.

For me Söderqvist's music also stirred memories of Ralph Vaughan Williams' score for Scott of the Antarctic (1948), Ennio Morricone's score for The Thing (1982) and some of Sibelius' tone poems – all of which, not coincidentally, evoke snow and ice. The only popular music in the film is used diegetically, issuing from radios or other audio devices, most memorably just prior to the swimming-pool massacre, in which Secret Service's 1982 synthpop hit 'Flash in the Night' plays on a transistor radio by the side of the pool. Elsewhere, sound effects provide important audio accompaniment, giving us information the images can not; footsteps in the snow, or Eli's stomach rumbling, the small change jingling in a victim's pocket as he's hoisted upside-down, or small girls screaming because they've spotted a dead body, or sounds coming from a neighbouring flat, or the muffled noises we hear when Oskar is being held underwater.

SPECIAL EFFECTS

Computer effects are used sparingly (the only scene in which they are really evident is the cat attack). When Oskar asks Eli how she reached his bedroom window, several floors up, she replies, 'I flew' and she isn't being whimsical. But we never actually see her in flight. Later, during the massacre, all the signs indicate that she is flying over the swimming-pool, dragging one of her victims across the surface of the water, but again, we don't see it directly. We glimpse the victim's kicking feet, but no more. The rest is left to our imaginations.

THE OTHER SWEDISH VAMPIRE MOVIE

WHAT A TOTALLY UNCOOL WAY TO DIE.

'Being a vampire has very many drawbacks.' Professor Beckert shows his true colours

It's useful to compare *Let the Right One In* with Anders Banke's *Frostbiten* (2006), the only other non-porn Swedish vampire movie to date. *Frostbiten* takes a larkier, more scattershot approach to the genre. Like *Let the Right One In*, it begins with snow falling (not exactly a coincidence, given Sweden's climate), but follows this with a prologue, set in Ukraine in 1944. Five soldiers from the German Army Scandinavian Volunteer Division, separated from their unit and lost, seek refuge in a seemingly uninhabited house in the forest, where they are attacked in the dark by a mysterious creature.

The prologue is played straight, but the serious tone is jettisoned once the film has jumped forward into the present. Annika Wallén and her daughter Saga arrive by car at a small town in Swedish Lapland which is to be their new home. Annika (who points out early on there will be 'no daylight for a month') starts work at the local hospital where Gerhard Beckert, 'a leading figure in genetic science', is dosing a coma victim with mysterious red capsules. At school, Saga meets a Goth girl called Vega, who invites her to a party. Lukas and Sebastian, a pair of fun-loving hospital interns who are first seen throwing syringes into an anatomy chart, steal some of the red capsules; Sebastian takes one and begins to turn into a vampire. Lukas, unaware of what has happened to his friend, spikes the punch at the party with the capsules, turning all the guests except Saga into vampires.

At the hospital, the coma patient wakes and bites Annika on the arm. Beckert (identified as one of the soldiers from the prologue) explains how he was bitten on the leg. After the war, he returned to Sweden and tried to find a cure for his condition ('Being a vampire has very many drawbacks'), but is now trying to develop a race of vampire-human hybrids. Annika destroys Beckert by stabbing him through the heart with part of a wooden broomhandle.

Saga manages to escape from the party. The police, who have been summoned by neighbours complaining about the noise, place her in an ambulance, which is driven away. The former coma patient, who is also in the back of the ambulance, calls Saga her sister. As the ambulance leaves town, driven by Annika, Saga looks in the rear-view mirror and sees her mother's eyes glowing red.

Frostbiten is a sloppy but mostly quite lively horror-comedy. Compared to the precision of *Let the Right One In*, much of the plotting, camerawork and framing seems arbitrary, and there are numerous scenes – such as a protracted discussion between Annika and Saga about a blue food mixer – which seem to serve no particular function other than as half-hearted attempts to convey a bond between mother and daughter. (There's so much inconsequential dialogue about the mixer, you half expect it to feature in a narrative pay-off later on, but it never does.) The characters in *Let the Right One In* make mistakes, but nobody acts like a complete idiot, whereas the plot of *Frostbiten* turns on not just one but repeated instances of people willingly swallowing a drug without knowing what it is or what its effects might be. Subsequent to the wartime prologue, the action doesn't appear to be taking place at any particular era; the pop cultural references (Iron Maiden, Def Leppard) could date from any time between the late 1970s and the present, nor do fashions and furnishing appear to belong to any specific era.

Vampirism is presented as a virus ('Similar to rabies, but a lot more aggressive') which can be communicated by both ingestion of contaminated material and biting, though the process doesn't seem to have been given much thought and varies from character to character according to the whim of the screenwriters; some characters transform quickly, others more gradually, and the absence of daylight is not really exploited the way it is in *30 Days of Night* (2007) in which a group of vampires descends on an isolated Alaskan town in midwinter for an all-you-can-eat buffet. There are other inconsistencies: Sebastian's mirror image disappears, yet Annika's does not.

*Death by gnome.
'What a totally
uncool way to die'*

A vampire impaled on a garden gnome ('What a totally uncool way to die'), and another speaking in a high-pitched voice after inhaling helium are played for broad laughs, as is the vampire's ability to hear dogs talking. We never learn whether the dogs really are talking, whether it's a consequence of the newly infected vampire's heightened senses or whether it's all in his mind; in films such as *Go* (1999) and *Smiley Face* (2007), the ability to hear animals speak is presented as a side-effect of drug use. *Frostbiten* also recycles many horror movie clichés, such as subjective camerawork from the point of view from the vampire stalking a victim. The first victim, a youth on a motorbike, is seen through red-tinged vampire-vision and dragged kicking into the air by something out of frame.

The vampires in *Frostbiten* have preternatural strength and appear to feel more at ease off the ground; they have a habit of crawling on ceilings, shinning up walls or lying in wait up lamposts. The most startling visual effect is a neighbour's eye view of vampires swarming up the sides of the party house; it's reminiscent of the moment in *Let the Right One In* where we see Eli scuttling up the exterior wall of the hospital like a dark spider, but in *Frostbiten* the effect is played for laughs, with a policewoman delivering the punchline, 'A woman called complaining about teenagers climbing the walls'.

Other clichés are so familiar they're impossible to take seriously: a vampire (Beckert) who transforms into a large naked creature (we never find out what happens to his clothes) like Gary Oldman in *Bram Stoker's Dracula* or Chris Sarandon in *Fright Night*, a vampire villain who is also a mad Nazi scientist (Beckert again) who rants like a megalomaniac Bond villain, 'When I'm done, our kind will rule over all of you, like the cattle you are!' This sense of superiority and entitlement is a recurring motif in modern vampire movies, and can also found in *Rise* (2007) in which Bishop, the chief vampire, declares, 'I choose to experience everything the world has to offer, in exchange for a few meaningless lives!' and in *Blade*, in which Deacon Frost sneers, 'Look at them. They're cattle - pieces of meat'. But *Let the Right One In*'s Eli, far from seeing humans as inferior or as blood bags to be plundered, appears to regret having to kill them to survive, and actually seems to envy the human qualities she sees in Oskar.

THE VAMPIRE'S ARRIVAL

AND WHEN HE CROSSED THE BRIDGE, THE PHANTOMS CAME TO MEET HIM.

What's black and white and red all over? The beginning of a Swedish vampire movie, perhaps? *Let the Right One In* begins with a black screen with simple white credits and the title of the film in red, the typography arranged in a configuration reminiscent of 1950s modernism, the era in which the housing estate which provides the film with its central setting was constructed. Black, white and red will be the predominant colours of the film. The black of night and the darkness of Eli's hair and eyes contrast with the light of Oskar's blondness and the snow and reflect the light and dark within their own personalities.

The red, of course, is the red of blood, which throughout the film will be used sparingly but effectively. Håkan wears a red polo-neck jumper to commit the first murder in the film, and later pokes at Jocke's corpse with a red pole – the same red pole which is later picked up by Oskar for use as a defensive weapon. While at his father's, Oskar appropriates a red fleece cardigan, which he brings back home with him. Jocke is wearing a red plaid jacket when Eli kills him, and Ginia wears a red jacket prior to Eli's attack. When Oskar visits Eli's flat, she puts on Håkan's red jumper (which of course is so big on her it's almost like a dress) and later, when she changes into one of Oskar's mother's dresses, it's a red plaid. Jimmy, Conny's brother and the chief torturer of Oskar at the swimming-pool, wears a red jacket and a red jumper - obviously he's doomed. In the very last scene, when Oskar is escaping with Eli on the train, his bag is red.

Frostbiten begins with falling snow, followed by snow stained with red blood when an offscreen soldier is shot. The first moving image in *Let the Right One In* is also that of snow falling. 'We tried to create the sound of snow falling... inside your head, it has a sound,' says Alfredson. And so the first sounds are the almost subliminal effect of that snow falling, the distant rumble of a train, and the tyres of a car on a slushy road surface.

The circumstances of the vampire's arrival play an important role in vampire cinema. There have been several films set in alternative realities where vampirism is at least partially acknowledged by the surviving human characters and is either considered 'normal' or has almost completely superceded humanity - *Blade, Perfect Creature* (2006),

Ultraviolet (2006), *Daybreakers* (2009). But these are not pure vampire movies – they're a hybrid of comic-book and the alternative universes of science fiction. In the traditional vampire film, we are only rarely transported directly into the world or the viewpoint of the vampire. In the traditional vampire film, the 'normal' world has to be established before the vampire intrudes to prey on, infect or otherwise disrupt the lives of the humans there. Sometimes humans stray temporarily into the world of the vampire and return to their own after having become infected. Or they bring the vampire back with them. The vampire is the outsider, the trespasser, the bringer of disease and death; he or she is representative of a darker reality, the contaminator of the everyday world.

The chasm between the two worlds – of human and vampire, light and dark, reality and nightmare – has never been more eloquently expressed than in FW Murnau's *Nosferatu, eine Symphonie des Grauens* (1922), which includes one of the most famous intertitles of all time, beloved by the surrealists, when the Jonathan Harker character is travelling to Count Orlok's castle: 'And when he crossed the bridge, the phantoms came to meet him'. These words imply that in order for the vampire to gain a foothold in the world of humans, the humans must meet him at least halfway. In the world of *Let the Right One In*, the darkness is already a part of the human world; it infiltrated it long ago, made Eli what she is. But the darkness would have no power in that world if the humans didn't invite it into their hearts – humans like Håkan and, later, Oskar.

Nosferatu, eine Symphonie des Grauens was the first *bona fide* Dracula film, an unofficial silent adaptation of Bram Stoker's story, with names changed because the studio was unable to obtain rights to the novel. Murnau's film established many of what would later become familiar conventions of vampire cinema – the thirst for blood, superstitious peasants, plagues of rats, the destructive power of sunlight and vampirism as a metaphor for disease. It also conveys the sexual power of Stoker's novel; Max Schreck's Graf Orlok may resemble a hideous walking cadaver with his bald head, pointy teeth and long fingernails, but from the first glimpse of his outrageously phallic-shaped castle in the Carpathians to the final scenes of Ellen, the self-sacrificing heroine, surrendering herself to him with an erotic abandon entirely lacking from her scenes with her human fiancé (subsequently husband), he's a potent symbol of the dark side of desire. Thus the first *bona fide* vampire film is a perverted love story between a human (Ellen) and a vampire (Orlok). Clearly, the relationship between a vampire and a human was always going to

Nosferatu: the hideous walking cadaver on its way to Wisborg

be a *different* sort of relationship. But is it as different from inter-human relationships as all that?

Like few vampire films since, *Nosferatu* evokes geographical distance – something which has been de-emphasised in subsequent adaptations as air travel and telecommunications have shrunk the globe. In the shots of the doomed ship Demeter being tossed around on a stormy ocean, there's a palpable sense of a contagion creeping ever closer to home, bridging the gap between normalcy and nightmare. From Varna, on the Black Sea, all the way round to the fictitious city of Wisborg in North Germany is an epic voyage at the best of times. *Let the Right One In*, on the other hand, is almost entirely set in the suburbs of Stockholm (with a couple of interludes in the Swedish countryside, when Oskar visits his father) with the supernatural elements absorbed seamlessly into a recognisable everyday urban reality. But Eli is still an outsider, leading a shadowy existence. She's a newcomer and an outsider, and it's her arrival that sets the story in motion; in effect we hear it before we see it, with the sound of the taxi's tyres.

Where does Eli come from? Where has she been living before? We don't know, but we assume her previous lifestyle was much like the one we see now; rootless, drifting from place to place, surviving but without taking much pleasure from it; one of the reasons she is drawn to Oskar is that he reminds her of what she has lost. Her world, her reality, is very different to that of the people who already live in Blackeburg, and her arrival there forms the focus of the film's first sequence and succinctly, with very little dialogue, introduces us to the main characters.

In *Nosferatu* and many versions of the Dracula story, especially those set in the days before air travel, the vampire arrives via the ocean, having fed off the crew during the voyage so the ship that docks is now devoid of human life, like a ghost vessel. In *Dracula 2000* (2000) (known as *Dracula 2001* in territories where it opened the following year) the vampire travels from London (the old world) to New Orleans (the new world) by aeroplane. But in *Let the Right One In*, the vampire arrives by car – in a taxi, accompanied by her father figure/assistant, Håkan. It's dark and there's no-one around; not surprising since there's snow on the ground and it's presumably too chilly for folk to be hanging around outside, unless they're walking the dog or en route to a specific destination.

The cab draws up in front of an apartment block in a working-class suburb of Stockholm called Blackeberg, the red brick buildings of which were the height of modernity when it was built, in 1952. About 30 years later, when *Let the Right One In* is set, the angular construction has become shabby and slightly seedy in the way of much modernist architecture: flat surfaces stained by the elements, depressing ranks of identical square windows and what would presumably be, weather permitting, a mugger's paradise of hidden walkways, flights of steps, underpasses and archways linking one courtyard to the next. So many places to lie in wait. It makes you wonder why vampires traditionally remain aloof in remote castles or old dark mansions to which their victims have to be enticed or delivered (the idea of a dial-a-victim delivery service catering to a vampire clientele is irresistible), when they could be living right in amongst their prey, surrounded by an easily accessible supply of nourishing snacks and dinners.

The first words in *Let the Right One In* are Oskar's, though he's out of frame when he says them. 'Squeal like a pig. So, squeal!' It's night time. We see his point of view as he looks out of his bedroom window at the snow-covered estate. His reflection appears in the window; he looks like a ghost child, already half lost to the real world. In this introductory sequence, he is shot mostly in reflection, or through glass, emphasising his introversion and alienation from the rest of the world.

Linqvist cites, 'The feeling of being alone in the night, waiting for something to happen... waiting for anyone to come through the darkness, to change things. That feeling was a very important starting point.'

Oskar is in underpants, skinny and albino-pale, with longish platinum blond hair. His colouring will obviously seem less striking to audiences in Scandinavian countries (where for genetic reasons, possibly connected to pigmentation compensating for a deficiency of sunlight, there has always been a high proportion of blonds) but to the rest of us he looks a little otherwordly, like a boy in a fairytale (Hans Christian Anderson's *The Snow Queen*, perhaps, or Edmund in *The Lion, The Witch and the Wardrobe*) whose fate it is to be kidnapped, seduced or corrupted by a supernatural being. We can tell immediately that he's sad and lonely because he's talking to himself. Behind him, on the wall, is a mural of a leafy and autumnal woodland glade, a rather optimistic evocation of a rural idyll. His room is furnished in generic 1970s–1980s Ikea style; not stylish, but functional and comfortable.

The next shot is from inside the taxi drawing up outside Oskar's building. There's a close up, from behind, of Håkan, a solidly-built, pock-marked middle-aged man in the back seat, who looks sideways at his fellow passenger, also shot from behind. Only her dark hair is visible. She is humming to herself, as though not really engaged in the practical details of what's going on; perhaps she's leaving them up all to Håkan, who smiles at her indulgently. The fact that we don't immediately see her face immediately places her in a position of power, but we have to wait until her meeting with Oskar for our first proper introduction.

The main musical theme starts up. It's not your typical horror movie theme, but wistful and romantic. Oskar places the palm of his hand on the window pane, as though trying to connect with his own reflection. It's then that he notices the taxi and sees Håkan open the car door for a dark-haired girl of about Oskar's age to climb out. It's almost as if Oskar's gesture has summoned the vampire into existence from the depths of his own troubled soul, as though his wishful thinking has brought him an imaginary friend with superpowers who will eventually turn out to be his champion, saviour and companion. But it's an imaginary friend with a dark side, who will demand a price. The film doesn't

Oskar alone: reflections of a ghost boy

31

spell out what that price is, but it leaves us wondering about it.

Oskar picks up a knife, thrusts with it as he turns away from the window and repeats, 'Squeal! Squeal like a pig!' He's already dreaming about getting his own back on the bullies who make his life a misery at school, though we have yet to meet them. Thus, his first sightings of Eli follow immediately on from his fantasies of violent revenge.

In *Daughters of Darkness* (1971), Harry Kümel's kinky, stylish and camp Belgo-Franco-German update of the Elizabeth Báthory myth, we first glimpse the vampire when she draws up outside a hotel on the seafront of off-season Ostend by car (a vintage Bristol) driven by her 'secretary', who turns to her and says, 'Let's hope we'll find something better here. I'm so tired.' (German actress Andrea Rau pronounces it as 'I'm so tart'.) Our first glimpse of her vampire 'employer' – Countess Elizabeth Báthory – is black and white and red: pale face and hair, scarlet lipstick, black hat with veil, black fur-trimmed garments. As she climbs out of the car, she says, 'I'll go in first. You look after the luggage, Ilona'. The inference is that they've been travelling for some time, searching for a safe haven. And that Ilona is a dogsbody, a servant, a drudge, there to do the heavy lifting.

In *Let the Right One In*, Eli goes directly into Oskar's building, without looking at Håkan, who (like Ilona) is left to deal with the luggage. It's a ritual they must have performed many times before, suggesting that she takes him for granted. For people who are moving house, Håkan and the girl don't have many belongings - just a couple of suitcases and some boxes. Like the vampires in *Near Dark* (1987), Eli is a nomad, who must be able to pack up and leave at a moment's notice. But she's also the vampire equivalent of Neil McCauley, the master-thief played by Robert De Niro in Michael Mann's cops and robbers movie *Heat* (1995), who says: 'A guy told me one time, "Don't let yourself get attached to anything you are not willing to walk out on in 30 seconds flat if you feel the heat around the corner".' McCauley and Eli, both operating well outside the law, will end up having to put this rule into practice.

The camera peers in through Oskar's window; the reflections of the building opposite are visible. Even when the camera moves in, it remains on the other side of the glass from Oskar, giving him a slightly ethereal quality as he hides the knife under his bed and lies down. He hears movement and voices coming through the wall from the flat next door. This is the first sign that the acoustic insulation between these flats is poor, making complete privacy difficult; neighbours are privy to each other's business whether they like it or not, and conversations can be heard, if not understood, through the walls. Count Dracula, in his vast and draughty castle, had no such problems. His nearest neighbours were miles away.

In a tilted shot, again from outside the building, Håkan can be seen covering the window of his new flat with what looks like a fashion poster and flattened-out cardboard cartons, probably the ones in which his and Eli's belongings were packed. Again, it's an act which he appears to have done many times before, and he's clearly not fussy about appearances. The Venetian blind is half down, skew-whiff; this is not the sign of houseproud tenants. The poster depicts a larger-than-life woman's face in close-up, forearm across her brow in a sort of I've-got-a-headache gesture, nails lacquered red, thumb pointing down. It's tempting to see the thumbs-down as a portent: there goes the neighbourhood.

There goes the neighbourhood

The next shot shifts so that Håkan and the window are in soft focus in the background. In sharp focus in close-shot in the foreground, a somewhat weary-looking and dishevelled middle-aged man (whose name, we later find out, is Lacke) is peeing into the snow; he has been drinking and either can't wait or can't be bothered to make it back to empty his bladder in the comfort and warmth of his own home. The openness of the place he has selected indicates he is beyond caring. He glances up and round, and glimpses Håkan in the window in the background, but apparently thinks nothing of it and turns back to zip up his fly with a shrug of his shoulders. But later on in the story, he will remember this moment and put two and two together.

The sequence and accompanying musical theme come to a close with a wide shot of this part of the housing estate. Lamps lit, no-one visible. The location, which is as much a character as the people in it, is sealing everyone in for the night.

Thus we have already been introduced to the film's four main players and, to a degree, their relationship to one another: the vampire, the vampire's assistant, the vampire's antagonist and the boy who will become the vampire's significant other. This opening is breathtaking in its economy. In effect, the whole scene has been an establishing sequence. With virtually no dialogue, it sets up three of the main settings of the films – Oskar's room, Eli's flat and the courtyard, the common ground where the two of them will later meet and interact. They haven't met face-to-face yet, but the cross-cutting has already established an emotional connection between them.

MEETING THE VAMPIRE

I CAN'T BE YOUR FRIEND.

Oskar's school is introduced by an establishing shot, framed by the entrance to an underpass; it's a recurring location. Throughout the film, establishing shots – whether of the block of flats, the gym, the hospital or simply trees – play a role more important than merely labelling the location, or even providing rhythmic punctuation, though they fill that role too; they also indicate whether it's day or night, which is more than usually crucial in a film in which one of the two central characters is obliged to remain in darkness. Often the passing of an entire day is conveyed with a single brief scene of Oskar in the classroom, or being bullied. As the story progresses, the daylight scenes seem to become even shorter, almost perfunctory, while the night-time – Eli's domain – become increasingly dominant.

Thus, the establishing shot of the school shows us it's daylight (albeit very overcast) and this shot is linked to the next with a voice-over, 'The police have ways to determine foul play...'. It's a policeman talking to Oskar's class about crime – visiting policemen apparently being a common occurrence in Swedish schools since it's something that both Alfredson and Lindqvist remember from their own childhoods. The policeman is talking about a body found in a burnt-out house; he asks what is intended to be a rhetorical question. How did the police know the man was already dead when the fire was set? Oskar, alone out of his class, eagerly raises his hand to reply, 'There was no smoke in the lungs of the person who died'. That a 12-year-old should be familiar with this snippet of forensic pathology already marks him out as distinct from his peers; the action takes place many years before television series such as *CSI: Crime Scene Investigation* (2000–) familiarised the general public with such details. The policeman, understandably, is a little surprised and asked him how he knew that. Oskar replies, 'I read a lot...'.

The boy sitting in front of Oskar turns and looks back at him with an expression of disdain. This is Conny, whom we meet again in the very next scene, backing Oskar up against the lockers in the corridor. Oskar, evidently accustomed to this sort of treatment, barely reacts, merely closing his eyes in resignation. Conny insults Oskar, calls him a pig and flicks the tip of his nose, hard, before running off with his two supporters, Martin and Andreas. Now we know where Oskar has picked up his 'Squeal like a pig' line. Is he a strange child who reads about grisly murders because he has no friends and is bullied, or is he friendless and bullied because he's a strange child who reads about grisly murders? No matter, because Oskar, thanks to his almost albino-like paleness and puny physique, seems born to be a victim, and his resigned attitude suggests he has been one for a long, long time.

Up close and personal: Conny bullies Oskar

Horror fans will automatically feel an affinity with Oskar; we're already fascinated by grisly murders and blood, and often made to feel outsiders in cultural terms, merely for being interested in a genre which is still so often denigrated or condemned as degenerate or even dangerous by the arbiters of taste. I'm prepared to bet, too, that most sensitive people – in other words, avid readers or anyone whose cultural tastes extend beyond the obvious – think of themselves as 'outsiders'. So, although we might not all have been bullied at school, we empathise with Oskar and his problems. There but for the grace of God go the rest of us.

The next shot is of Oskar coming home, pausing in front of his building and looking up at the window next to his bedroom, the one we've seen Håkan covering with the poster and cardboard. Has he already guessed this is where Eli lives? The scene jumps straight to the interior of the flat on the other side of that window; Oskar can't see inside, but the next shots are close-ups of Håkan's hands as he prepares his 'murder kit' and packs it into a large briefcase as a radio announcer reads the weather forecast. It's first of many direct cuts between Oskar and Håkan, binding their fates together even though they never actually meet face to face on screen.

In Lindqvist's novel, Håkan is unambiguously a paedophile – a former teacher who was fired from his job and became a vagrant until 'rescued' by Eli; he loves Eli, who gives him money to find blood for her, but she refuses him the physical intimacy he desires. In the film, Lindqvist and Alfredson deliberately play down this aspect of the character, and were wise to do so, since paedophilia is such an emotive subject it would have distracted from the central relationship and become a film about child abuse instead of a vampire love story.

'I didn't want him to be just a monster,' says Lindqvist, and he's not – Håkan is all too human. In the film, his true nature and proclivities are left ambiguous, for the viewer to guess, and while he is still a despicable character (he kills without qualm) he's also pathetic, so obviously at the mercy of his feelings for Eli; without in any way condoning his actions, we feel sorry for him, and also find him slightly absurd. There's another reason for playing down the paedophilia, and it's this; the relationship between Eli and Håkan is already implicitly mimicking the pattern of a paedophile and a young girl, but with the roles reversed. Instead of the paedophile having 'groomed' the girl to be his companion, it's she who is the older by a couple of centuries, in which case it's more likely that she has 'groomed' him, and not the other way round. This is a notion which teeters distastefully on the edge of one of the paedophile's perennial bogus justifications for his egocentric desires – that the young child is more mature and sexually aware than he or she may appear, and is thus knowingly encouraging the paedophile's delusions.

The first murder in the film takes place in a snowy park full of silver birches in Vällingby, two metro stops away from Blackeberg. It's getting dark, and the lamps in the park are already lit. Håkan steps into frame and accosts a passing youth, asking him the time. The youth is curious about the gas mask and canister Håkan is holding. Håkan explains that the canister contains halothane, a colourless, pleasant-smelling vapour used in general anaesthetic. He forces the youth to inhale it, knocking him unconscious. All this is shown in long shot, with the action partially obscured by trees.

A snowy park full of silver birches: Håkan and his victim

In the next shot, the camera glides sideways through the trees and the strange squeaking we hear is revealed, in a medium shot, as the sound of Håkan hauling the unconscious youth upside down with a system of rope and pulleys, suspending him from a tree. Håkan, who is now wearing a see-through plastic mac over his clothes, is panting with the effort; small change jingles in the victim's pocket. We see Håkan readying the plastic can and funnel, but he obscures our view as he slits the boy's throat. Then there's an extreme, almost abstract close-up of blood running into the can, some of it dribbling down the outside, accompanied by the sound effects of liquid trickling into a plastic receptacle.

A large white poodle bounds into the frame; offscreen, its owner calls 'Ricky!' Ricky the poodle stops and barks at Håkan and refuses to budge, even when he tries to drive it off by throwing snow at it. There's a deadpan comic moment as Håkan and the dog look at one another before Håkan panics, knocks over the cannister and forgets both the blood and the funnel as he gathers up his belongings and, with the imprecation 'Stupid dog!', flees out of frame. Ricky's owner and a friend, both young women, arrive on the scene and look suitably shocked. The dog provides the scene with a dark punchline as it starts licking the blood on the ground.

With the exception of the cut between Håkan gassing the youth and beginning to string him upside-down, the murder sequence is played out in real time, with virtually no dialogue. Its very matter-of-factness is horrific – Håkan shows no hesitation in killing, and it's evidently not the first time he has taken a life. But the horror is counterbalanced by grim humour; the fact that the dog is a standard poodle, with the classic poodle cut, adds a touch of surrealism. Poodles are generally thought of as pampered pets, not drinkers of blood (though Mephistopheles disguises himself as a black poodle in Goethe's *Faust*). There's a poodle in *Frostbiten* too, but there it falls victim to the vampire instead of driving off the vampire's helper.

Håkan's clumsiness is amusing, and might almost be endearing if he were not engaged on such a ghastly mission. This is no merciless killing machine, like Michael Myers or Jason Vorhees, the serial-killers of slasher movie franchises *Halloween* (1978) and *Friday the 13th* (1980). Håkan is all too evidently human, and fallible.

While there's nothing yet directly tying Eli to the murder, we assume, since we've seen her with Håkan, that she is somehow tied to it. A viewer coming to the film for the first time, with no foreknowledge or awareness of its genre, could conceivably conclude that Eli is ignorant of her companion's activities, but it's doubtful. Even before we've seen the murder in the park, there's already something odd about this couple and their relationship. There can be few viewers who haven't by now guessed that Eli is a vampire.

The scene is now set for the first meeting between our two protagonists. Oskar is the first to arrive, emerging from the entrance to his building and, after a quick look around, extracting his knife from the inside pocket of his jacket. He keeps it in a sheath, and looks at it proudly. It's another of the links between him and Håkan, who in the last scene was seen preparing to slit the youth's throat with a large knife. Would Oskar ever be capable of slitting someone's throat for Eli, as Håkan has done?

He's certainly prepared to stab a tree. Oskar trudges through the snow (as Kim Newman has pointed out, the 'packed snow means any exterior scenes have to involve *trudging*, while being wrapped up against the cold prevents the uniformly self-involved, depressed adults from making connections') and approaches a tree as though it were a person, before challenging it – 'What are you staring at? Well? Are you looking at me? Well, fuck off! What's your problem? Are you scared? So, scream! Squeal!' – before stabbing at it with his knife. It's Oskar's *Taxi Driver* (1976) moment: the monologue and accompanying aggressive posturing of a put-upon loner which echoes the scene where Travis Bickle (Robert De Niro) says 'You talking to me?' at his own reflection, rehearsing his own tough guy stance and imagining a confrontation.

I daresay we all talk to ourselves in the mirror from time to time, or even swear at inanimate objects when they don't behave the way we'd like them to. But pretending a tree is a person and threatening it, as a sort of dry run or rehearsal for what one would like to do in real life, is unusually eccentric behaviour. In Oskar's fantasy world, he's a powerful killer, out for vengeance on the kids who make his life a misery. Which is precisely when Eli, as if in answer to his subconscious prayers, comes into his life.

Psychothrillers are full of characters who represent the protagonist's evil id – that part of him (only rarely is it a her) which performs those actions the protagonist is prevented from doing by social inhibition, morality or physical weakness or cowardice, but which advances his cause by removing obstacles or irritations or pandering to an idealised self-image. Bruno in *Strangers on a Train* (1951), Alex in *Bad Influence* (1990), Harry in *Harry, He's Here to Help* (2000) are three such characters. Sometimes, as in *Psycho* (1960) or *Fight Club* (1999), the other character turns out to be a literal alter-ego, an integral part of the protagonist's own personality. The progenitors of such stories are James Hogg's *The Private Memories and Confessions of a Justified Sinner* (1824), in which a young man is tempted by his doppelgänger into committing a series of offences, including murder, and its more famous successor, Robert Louis Stevenson's *Strange Case of Dr Jekyll and Mr Hyde* (1886), in which Dr Jekyll devises a potion which unleashes his evil id. The doctor's shapeshifting, which transforms him into a swarthy, thick-set alter ego without inhibitions, is an expression of 'the thorough and primitive duality of man' (*Dr Jekyll and Mr Hyde and Other Stories*, Penguin 1979, p 82), as Dr Jekyll puts it. The inference is that the inhibitions imposed upon us by society prevent us from revealing our true selves, but since these selves would thus be unleashed to indulge in aggressive or antisocial behaviour, unfettered self-expression is not always an admirable thing.

During their first meeting, Oskar and Eli share the frame, but there is always distance between them. Eli's first sight of Oskar must be when he's stabbing the tree, which is perhaps enough to pique her interest in him as a person as opposed to a possible food source. As we will later see, when she goes in for the kill, it's quick and without preamble, so it seems she has already discounted Oskar as prey. Or perhaps the courtyard is simply too exposed for use as a hunting ground.

LET THE RIGHT ONE IN

Oskar senses someone behind him; the camera turns with him to see: Eli, standing perfectly still on top of the jungle gym, a small climbing frame in the middle of the courtyard which is to become their regular meeting place. She's wearing an oversized shirt with the sleeves rolled up and trousers, but no jacket, scarf or hat, the lack of which already marks her out as different in the Swedish climate. 'What are you doing?' she asks. 'Nothing,' he replies before asking her the same question. 'Nothing,' she replies. When Oskar asks, 'Do you live here?', she takes the question literally, and replies, 'Yeah, I live right here, in the jungle gym'. It's not such a mendacious answer; Eli has no real home, and really does live wherever she happens to be, in the moment, without ties. Oskar repeats his question, and Eli indicates her window and tells him they're next-door neighbours. Eli jumps down from the climbing frame, takes a few steps towards Oskar and says, 'Just so you know, I can't be your friend'. Then she goes inside; Oskar gazes after her, obviously intrigued, and belatedly asks (just as we always come up with the perfect retort when it's too late): 'Are you so sure that I want to be your friend?'

It's Eli who first brings up the subject of friendship, which indicates it must already have crossed her mind. Maybe she has already divined that Oscar is lonely and desperate for companionship. (Talking to trees is a bit of a giveaway.) Perhaps she recognises him as potential friend material.

As if in reply, the film cuts directly from Oskar in the snowy courtyard to Håkan on a subway train (another of the many cuts between the two characters). He's sitting, with a blank facial expression, next to his bundled up bloodstained plastic mac; it's only when he makes a move to put it away in his briefcase that he realises he has forgotten the plastic canister with the blood. There's an abrupt cut to a medium-shot of Eli, shown from neck to thigh, out of focus and in the background, angrily flinging the balled-up plastic mac at the open case, with Håkan looking impassive in the foreground. 'You're supposed to help me!' she says, and moves across the foreground, a shadowy figure, still out of focus. 'Do I really have to take care of this myself?' At this point she seems to be facing him directly, and though he doesn't move or change his expression, he seems almost to be bracing himself. Though we never see Eli's face, it's obvious she is in a rage, a complete contrast to her mood in the previous scene. Her breathing is ragged. She shouts, 'Say something!'

Håkan, still looking strangely impassive, says, 'Forgive me.' It could almost be a mundane domestic dispute, with an angry wife berating her husband for coming home without the ingredients he was supposed to pick up for dinner.

An out-of-focus Eli berates Håkan for failing to bring home the blood

The next shot is in daylight; Oskar's teacher is talking about the previous evening's murder, and reminding the children that counselling is available. Conny raises a laugh by asking glibly, 'Is it all right to kill the killer if you happen to meet him?' He's already advocating an eye for an eye, which will be echoed in his older brother's demand of 'an eye for an ear' at the film's climax. When Oskar eventually hits back, Conny will hit back even harder, only to be hit back harder still when Eli actively intervenes on Oskar's side.

Conny can't foretell all this, of course. After class, Oskar hides in a toilet cubicle to avoid him. We assume he hides there for quite some time, until after the bullies have given up and gone home, because in the next scene his mother is scolding him, insisting he come straight home after school and not stray from the courtyard. (The irony is, of course, that Oskar has already met a killer there.) While she's talking on the phone, Oskar grabs a newspaper and shuts himself in his room to read about the murder. Like a fan collecting details about his favourite film star, he cuts out the article to add to a scrapbook of cuttings about massacres and pictures of knives. This is visual confirmation of what we already gathered from Oskar's display of forensic knowledge in class - that his thoughts are already of death and blood, even before he knows what Eli is.

Massacres and pictures of knives: Oskar's murder scrapbook

Like all the adults in the film, with the possible exception of Mr Avila, the Spanish physical education teacher, Oskar's mother is oblivious to the realities of her son's life. She's neither neglectful nor cruel, and provides him with all the necessary home comforts, but as a single parent she's clearly got her hands full providing for him and fails to engage with him on an emotional level. There are two interludes in the narrative when Oskar spends the weekend with his father in his house in the country. (The first goes swimmingly; the second will not go so well.) Oskar and his father ride snowbikes and play noughts and crosses, but the father behaves more like a playmate than a parent, and clearly it's the mother who looks after Oskar in practical ways, though both parents are so wrapped up in themselves they fail to recognise either the loneliness of their son, the fact that he's being bullied or, once he has made friends with Eli, the visible change in his character. Like Oskar's teachers, they're looking elsewhere and failing to see what's going on under their noses.

It's here that we're introduced to another group of adults who will play important roles in the story: the drinking buddies at The Sun Palace, a Chinese cafe on the ground floor of another part of the housing estate. Lacke, whom we've already seen urinating, is there with his girlfriend Virginia (whom he calls Ginia) and a couple of others, including Jocke, who will fall victim to Eli at the end of the evening. They're all a bit pickled, grumbling about the government, the murder and capital punishment; there's a sense they spend most of their lives sitting around here, drinking and smoking. Håkan is sitting by himself at a table by the window, drinking milk. Politely but a little off-handedly, he rebuffs Lacke's invitation for him to join the group. 'You don't have to sit here all alone, join us and have a laugh,' Lacke remarks as Håkan pays his bill and prepares to leave. 'No thanks,' says Håkan, 'I'm in a hurry'. It's the only direct contact the two men have with each other in the film, but establishes the fact that Lacke is aware of Håkan, knows he is a newcomer and has just moved in with his daughter. But Håkan, of course, can't afford to make friends. Unlike Eli, who's in the process of making one.

RUBIK'S CUBE: THE SECOND MEETING

I MIGHT NOT BE HERE TOMORROW.

Sharing his toys: Oskar hands over the Rubik's Cube

Oskar's second meeting with Eli takes place, like their first encounter, on the jungle gym. He's playing with his Rubik's Cube, as though having instinctively selected an object he thinks might intrigue the newcomer. (The Rubik's Cube is a puzzle-toy comprising interlocking plastic pieces, and first went on sale in 1980.) Lindquist says the cube is a 'homage to Clive Barker' and represents a means of 'getting in touch with the other side'. In *Hellraiser* (1987) (adapted from Barker's short story *The Hellbound Heart*) and its sequels, the Lament Configuration is a cube-shaped puzzle which, when solved, opens a gateway to another dimension of pain, desire and delirium, through which demons can pass into our world.

In the second meeting, the physical distance between Oskar and Eli has decreased. Once again, he's already there when she arrives. They're both sitting on the climbing frame this time, though she's above him on the frame. In this scene, there are more close-ups than during Oskar and Eli's first meeting, but never one in which they're together in sharp focus at the same time. At this point in the story, they're still feeling their way towards each other.

Eli looks even more unkempt than before. Her fingernails are filthy. Because of her inappropriate clothing and apparent lack of rudimentary hygiene, a child more socially integrated than Oskar would surely have steered clear of her; perhaps Eli feels drawn to him simply because she's accustomed to other children avoiding her.

Eli notices the Rubik's Cube, and Oskar's instincts are proved right, because she is immediately curious, asking, 'Is it some kind of puzzle?' Oskar asks her if she'd like to try; it's the first big overture of friendship, the child unselfishly sharing his toys. 'You can give it back tomorrow,' he says, to which she replies cryptically, 'I might not be here tomorrow'. Oskar is not fazed; 'The day after, then,' he says. As she plays with the cube, Oskar observes, 'You smell funny'. An adult would never say something so direct and potentially insulting, but Oskar hasn't yet learned to dissemble like an adult. He also asks her why she doesn't feel the cold, to which Eli's answer is, 'I guess I've forgotten how'.

Oskar absorbs this information without really understanding it, but doesn't push his luck with further questioning. He says, 'See you tomorrow,' and goes indoors. From his point of view this has been a successful meeting; he has held up his side of the conversation without being humiliated, or sneered, or laughed at. He has met someone who neither nags nor bullies him, and who, unlike adults, seems interested in what he's doing. His questions have been taken seriously and the replies to them have apparently been honest, and he has succeeded in his aim to pique the interest of the newcomer.

What Oskar doesn't see, as he leaves, is that Eli is bent over with abdominal cramps. Her stomach is still making a loud rumbling noise, a sounds which recurs throughout the film whenever she's hungry, and in need to blood. She has a look of sad desperation on her face and lets out a sigh. If she'd been thinking of drinking Oskar's blood, she would have done it here. Instead, it's immediately after this meeting that she attacks and kills Jocke (see 'The Vampire as Serial Killer').

Oskar, though, is unaware of this. In the morning, he finds the completed Rubik's Cube on the jungle gym and smiles. We hear a bird singing. It's a message of hope.

There's a cut to Eli, sleeping peacefully, then back to Oskar in class, holding the Rubik's Cube under his desk. The editing, and the cube, have established a connection between them. He's happy. His world has been transformed. The lonely boy has found an ally.

HITTING BACK: THE THIRD MEETING

HIT BACK. HARD.

Sharing the frame: together, in focus, for the first time

When Oskar meets Eli for the third time, she's already waiting for him on the jungle gym, in contrast to the first two meetings, when it was she who joined him there. She looks healthier, and asks, 'Do I smell better now?' (Since their last meeting, of course, she has satisfied her hunger by drinking Jocke's blood.) It's at this point they introduce themselves to each other formally, with an exchange of names. Eli gives her age as 'Twelve... more or less'. Which means they're the same age, more or less, though Oskar finds it inconceivable that someone of their age wouldn't know exactly, as he does: 'Twelve years, eight months and nine days.' He also finds it odd that she doesn't know her date of birth, and, concluding she doesn't get birthday presents, offers her the Rubik Cube as a gift. She declines the offer, but shows him how to solve the puzzle.

For the first time, they're sharing the frame, sitting side by side, both in focus simultaneously. As she's playing with the cube, his gaze momentarily drifts off to one side, behind her, as if not so much focusing on what she's doing as finding it difficult to believe he's actually sitting here, engaged in a harmless pastime, with a child of his own age. It's as though he can't believe his luck. As if this is the first time he has found himself in this situation.

The next day, Oskar stays behind after class to copy the Morse code from an encyclopedia. When he leaves, he's confronted outside school by Conny and his minions. At Conny's urging, Andreas hits Oskar's legs with a stick. Oskar is obviously in pain but otherwise doesn't react, perhaps thinking it best to get the ordeal over with as soon as possible. Martin takes the stick and hits Oskar across the face with it, cutting his cheek. The three bullies realise they risk getting into trouble, and run off, mockingly calling their victim's name.

This scene is perhaps the most shocking in the film. Up till this point, the bullying has seemed more psychological than physical, but now we're made aware of the extent of the torments Oskar is obliged to confront on a daily basis. It's a vile, cowardly attack – three against one. All of a sudden, Oskar seems braver and less puny to the viewer; day after day he continues to attend school, knowing all too well the sort of thing that might be in store for him. Not only does he not cry from either pain or humiliation (throughout the attack, Andreas and Martin appear more upset than he is) but he doesn't snitch to teachers or parents. Later, he explains the cut on his face by telling his mother he tripped over a rock, and she's too precoccupied (her head, appropriately, is out of frame here) to divine the truth, or to wonder precisely what kind of tumble would result in such a clean slice across the cheek.

By contrast, when he meets Eli later on to teach her Morse code (this time we see neither of them arriving, but jump directly from Oskar at the supper table to the two children on the climbing frame), Eli notices the sticking-plaster and understands immediately what happened. All he has to say is, 'Some classmates...'. Eli, who knows all about being a victim, looks at him seriously and says, 'Hit back. Hard'. Oskar's mother and teachers may have failed him as protectors and guardians, but Eli does not. She says: 'Hit harder than you dare. Then they'll stop.' And when he says, 'What if...?' she says, firmly: 'Then I'll help you. I can do that.'

After a couple of centuries of fending for herself, Eli is an expert at violence and its consequences. The atrocity to which she was subjected right at the start of her career as a vampire (in the novel, there's a flashback to his/her genital mutilation at the hands of a Gilles de Rais-type character) was a form of extreme victimisation. It's not even particularly wise or useful advice she gives Oskar, since the consequence of his hitting back will be an escalation of the violence against him. But it's the only advice Eli knows how to give, and she's right in that she really can 'do that'.

When she says, 'Then I'll help you,' she places her hand on his. Throughout their first three meetings, they've been getting closer – almost but not quite touching while exchanging the Rubik's Cube or tapping out Morse code letters – but only now, in the fourth, is there direct physical contact between them, sealing the deal that will ultimately bring Eli to Oskar's rescue in the swimming-pool, though not before he has saved her bacon first. Unseen by either of them, Håkan is watching them from his window. Returning to the flat, Eli tells him with unthinking cruelty, 'You're in the way,' before turfing him out of the room where he's lounging on the blankets he uses as a bed, reading a magazine, so she can get at the party wall and tap messages to Oskar in Morse code, turning her back on Håkan, who is now ousted from his position in her life. He is indeed 'in the way' and he knows it. Eli and her new friend have even developed a private means of communication – in the form of the Morse Code – from which Håkan is ruthlessly excluded.

The rhythm of the film is accelerating, skipping more rapidly through the daylight scenes, which provide brief punctuation between Oskar's meetings with Eli after dark. Even when he's apart from her in the daytime, he's usually doing something which connects the two of them – holding the Rubik's Cube in class, copying out Morse code, or – as he is now – following her advice by signing up for weight-training to build up his phsyical strength.

That evening, Oskar buys candy at a sweet-shop while Eli waits outside; it's the first time we've seen them together away from the jungle gym. This is progress in their relationship – even something vaguely resembling a date. The shop's cat hisses violently at Eli through the window – an early sign that cats don't like vampires, and a foreshadowing of the cat attack on Virginia later on. When Oskar offers his bag of sweets to Eli, she initially turns him down, then changes her mind and eats one. Either she's in momentary denial and pretending to herself that she's a normal child after all, like Oskar, or she eats the sweet deliberately, knowing all the while that it will make her vomit (which it duly does) but simply wanting to do something that normal children do. After she throws up, Oskar's response is to hug her, rather awkwardly. She looks taken aback, then wistful, and asks, 'Oskar, do you like me?'

He says, 'Yeah, a lot,' to which she responds, 'If I wasn't a girl, would you like me anyway?' Oskar replies that he supposes so, and adds, 'Why do you ask?' But she's not ready to go there, not just yet. By this stage, the audience assumes that when she implies that she isn't a girl, she means she's a vampire. The reality, as we will see, is even more complicated.

THE VAMPIRE'S APPEARANCE

> The body undergoes remarkable changes in both size and color after death, and these are unlikely to enhance its attractiveness. (*Vampires, Burial, and Death*, Paul Barber, Yale University Press, 1988, p103)

Barber goes on to itemise these changes in his book. If the corpse is supine, the blood will have drained downwards, impelled by gravity, so that the face 'is likely to be pallid' (p105). (If the corpse is prone, however, the opposite will hold true, and the face will be suffused with blood, and will darken.) Changes due to bacterial action, seepage of blood into other parts of the body, putrefaction and saponification can all result in or contribute to discolouration. However, there are a number of conditions which can lead to a body which does not decompose in the normal way, which sometimes resulted in superstitious peoples attempting to account for such seemingly unnatural phenomena with explanations pertaining to the supernatural (Barber's examples date from the sixteenth, seventeenth and eighteenth centuries in Silesia, Greece and Kosovo).

Gases which bloat the corpse, skin slippage which reveals what is apparently a 'new' skin, the emission of blood-stained fluid from the mouth and nose might all be interpreted by the superstitious as the result of the dead person having become a vampire. Unrecognised diseases, epidemics and unexplained death might all be blamed on this creature. Barber writes: 'Our descriptions of revenents and vampires match up, detail by detail, with what we know about dead bodies that have been buried for some time' (p118).

If the vampire myth has its origins in the superstitions of mediaeval peasants faced with grotesque manifestations of disease and decomposition, how did the twenty-first century movie vampire end up as such a dazzlingly attractive creature – literally so in the case of *Twilight*'s Edward Cullen, who glitters in sunlight – with superhuman strength and sex appeal? And why does this make the character of Eli so different from other contemporary movie vampires?

Since the cadaverous Count Orlok in *Nosferatu*, the movies have tended to overlook the vampire's origins in East European myths as a means of accounting for post-mortem movement and growth in decaying corpses distended by gases, changes in colour and so on. Mina Harker, in her journal in Stoker's *Dracula*, describes the Count as, 'a tall, thin man, with a beaky nose and black moustache and pointed beard... His face was not a good face; it was hard, and cruel, and sensual, and his big white teeth, that looked all the whiter because his lips were so red, were pointed like an animal's' (*Dracula*, Bram Stoker, 1897/Penguin 1979, p207). Curiously, Dracula is invariably portrayed in the movies as clean-shaven (though Christopher Lee sports a moustache in Jesus Franco's *Count Dracula* [1970] and Gary Oldman has a rather dashing tash- and-goatee combo in *Bram Stoker's Dracula*).

Dracula is the most famous vampire of them all, an instantly recognisable cultural icon, or cliché, on a par with James Bond or Sherlock Holmes. He is always smartly dressed, as befits a Count. Todd Browning's *Dracula* (1931), the first talkie to be released with that title, wasn't adapted directly from the novel, but from Hamilton Deane's stage version of it, which is perhaps why the results seem more stilted than the silent but more visually adventurous *Nosferatu*. But the early, eerie scenes in Dracula's castle are exquisitely photographed by Karl Freund, who had formerly collaborated in Germany with F.W. Murnau and Fritz Lang. Additions to the vampire movie rulebook include Dracula's ability to turn himself into a bat, an aversion to crucifixes and a full complement of classic one-liners, some drawn directly from Stoker's novel ('Listen to them! Children of the night – what music they make!'). Dwight Frye's Renfield usurps the narrative functions of Jonathan Harker's character in the story before ending up in the asylum, eating spiders and babbling about the master.

The cast is dominated, of course, by Bela Lugosi, who first played the role on stage and is the very incarnation of a menacing but seductive foreigner - Rudolph Valentino's evil id. Lugosi's portrayal also established classic vampire garb in the popular imgaination: tuxedo and cape (which in Hammer's Technicolor Dracula films sometimes had a scarlet lining) which can be extended by the arms to somewhat resemble the wings of a large bat, a scallop effect echoed in a widow's peak hairline, most pronounced in Eddie, the young vampire son in the TV comedy series *The Munsters* (1964–6). The widow's peak effect also echoes the sharp point of the vampire's fangs. It's Lugosi's Dracula who is referenced in vampire spoofs, and in *Sesame Street*, the breakfast cereal Count Chocula and the cartoon series *Count Duckula* (1988–93).

Since 1931, the character of Dracula appeared in hundreds of films and TV shows, including a Spanish language version of Browning's *Dracula*, (shot back-to-back with it and on the same sets, but with a Spanish-speaking cast) and the broadly comic *Abbot and Costello Meet Frankenstein* (1948). But in the vast majority of these, it's still Lugosi's interpetation providing the blueprint: tuxedo and cape, East European accent, heavy foreign menace. In modern times, with the increasing scarcity of occasions demanding formal wear, this is not a vampire who would blend easily into a crowd, unless it was gathering on Halloween. Nowadays, it would be assumed that a man dressed like Lugosi was in fancy dress – dressed up as Count Dracula, in fact.

The first major challenger to Lugosi as the definitive movie vampire was Christopher Lee in Terence Fisher's *Dracula* (1958), made in the UK by Hammer Film Productions, which the previous year had already revived and reworked Frankenstein and his monster in *The Curse of Frankenstein* (1957). Hammer's first vampire movie brought Stoker's villain home to the British Isles where he was first conceived (albeit a British Isles which was pretending to be somewhere in mittel-Europe) and added colour; Lee's chin is stained, post-feed, with trickles of vivid scarlet blood. Other fresh elements include visible fangs. Lee speaks with an English accent, and is taller and more physically alluring than the chunky Lugosi; the vampire still has some way to go before he can blend into the modern world, and his appearance, though urbane, is merely a leaner, meaner variation on the Lugosi model, but if Lee's Dracula were to set up home in, say, a drab suburb of Stockholm, he would still attract a great deal of unwelcome attention.

Hammer's Dracula is manifestly evil, but the sexuality of the vampire is made more explicit by the orgiastic responses of his female victims, who often seem to welcome his attentions and are transformed by his bite from prim English matrons into sensual beings whose heaving bosoms, parted lips and fevered glances leave us in no doubt as to the nature of their desire. In *Dracula*, Terence Fisher's stately, atmospheric direction, Jimmy Sangster's screenplay and Bernard Robinson's lush production design set the style for all subsequent Hammer vampire yarns – dark fairy-tales invariably filmed in the parkland surrounding Bray Studios, Hammer's Home Counties HQ, but a long way

Count Dracula, the archetypal movie vampire (clockwise from top left): Bela Lugosi, Christopher Lee and Gary Oldman's Dracula as an old man; in Bram Stoker's Dracula

from the reality of a post-war Britain only a few years after the end of rationing. These are rigorously moralistic stories in which Good defeats Evil; the vampire's influence is countered by learned patriarchal figures such as Peter Cushing's Van Helsing who, backed up by church and family, and armed with academic knowledge and anti-vampire paraphenalia, defeats the vampire, and restores order and the status quo.

Hammer introduced fangs and red contact lenses to the vampire repertoire. But two early 1980s horror comedies which played an important role in the evolution of the vampire film weren't about vampires at all. Both *The Howling* (1981) and *An American Werewolf in London* (1981) featured groundbreaking scenes in which men are transformed into werewolves before the very eyes of the audience in on-screen special effects sequences depicting the painful-looking man-into-wolf process in excruciating detail: fingernails growing into claws, hands and feet stretching into lupine paws, the rippling of flesh as hair sprouts from it, and the crackling of bones as the skeleton reconfigures beneath the skin. The resulting creatures, though not entirely lupine, are a long way from Lon Chaney Jr's ingrowing dentures and dog-faced jowls in *The Wolf Man* (1941).

Naturally, vampire films weren't to be outdone by their werewolf cousins in the special effects department, but although Christopher Lee's fangs and red contact lenses would shortly seem very restrained compared to the prosthetic and, later, CGI monsters that were soon to become *de rigueur*, vampire films lagged behind werwolves until *Vamp* (1986). Grace Jones plays a vampire stripper called Katrina, whose pre-transformation appearance on stage – orange wig, whiteface make-up and Keith Haring-style bodypaint – already makes her seem like an unearthly being before, on the point of feeding, she finally morphs into a toothy creature with long fingernails who looks more like a werewolf than a vampire. At the climax of *Fright Night*, Chris Sarandon's vampire-next-door turns from an urbane man-about-town into a monster with bad skin, a mouthful of oversized teeth and blazing yellow eyes and thereafter changes in rapid succession into a giant killer-bat, a wolfish burn victim which explodes in green flames, and a crumbling skeleton. In *Bram Stoker's Dracula*, the title character (played by Gary Oldman) can transform into a wolf, green mist or rats, while his human appearance ranges from mummified Chinese mandarin with a Princess Leia hair-do to dapper Victorian gent in top hat and sunglasses.

As for the female vampire, Stoker gives a particularly vivid description which includes a virtual blueprint for the special effects transformations in vampire films of the 1980s onwards. Van Helsing and his companions visit Lucy Westenra's tomb and find it empty, but she then appears, 'dressed in the cerements of the grave...we recognised the features of Lucy Westenra. Lucy Westenra, but yet how changed. The sweetness was turned to adamantine, heartless cruelty, and the purity to voluptuous wantonness' (*Dracula*, Bram Stoker, 1897/Penguin 1979, p252). Her beauty seems to hypnotise Arthur Holmwood, her erstwhile fiancé, but when Van Helsing springs forward with a crucifix:

[the] beautiful colour became livid, the eyes seem to throw out sparks of hell-fire, the brows were wrinkled as though the folds of the flesh were the coils of Medusa's snakes, and the lovely, blood-stained mouth grew to an open square, as in the passion masks of the Greeks and Japanese. If ever a face meant death – if looks could kill – we saw it at that moment. (p254)

Eli never dresses in the sort of long white floaty gowns traditionally associated with female vampires. She rather resembles the vampires from *Martin* or *Near Dark* in that she tries to pass for normal, without taking much pride or care in her appearance or personal hygiene. She has many of the abilities of traditional vampires, including some of the supernatural ones such as flying and super-strength, but like the nomadic blood-drinkers of *Near Dark*, she is not technically dead. (When Oskar later asks directly, 'Are you dead?' she replies, 'No. Can't you tell?') Eli drinks blood, but as far as we can see doesn't have fangs. (In the novel, she invites Oskar to feel her teeth, and a witness to the swimming-pool massacre describes her as having 'the kind of teeth like a lion' [Lindqvist, 2008, p518].) She looks like a neglected child, either a homeless orphan or a girl left by parents to her own devices. Her clothing appears selected by default, put on for propriety rather than style or necessity; an odd assortment of shirts and sweaters (some so big they probably belong to Håkan, who evidently has no more sense of style than she does) and trousers, and it's established early on she doesn't feel the cold; she can go barefoot in the snow without, apparently, getting chilblains. Her hair is stringy and unkempt, as though she rarely bothers to wash or comb it, and though obviously she has to clean herself up after a kill has left her covered with blood, it doesn't seem to her a matter of urgency; when she climbs in through Oskar's window after drinking Håkan's blood, she hadn't bothered to clean the blood off her face, though she does make sure Oskar doesn't see it.

As Oskar observes, she stinks; her body odour apparently improves after she has fed, though his reaction indicates not by much. When he enters her flat for the first time, one can see from his expression that it too smells bad. It's odd that few vampire movies have broached the subject of what a vampire might smell like; rotting corpses by definition wouldn't have a pleasant odour, while an all-blood diet wouldn't be likely to result in sweet-scented breath. And what about hygiene? In those versions of the myth where running water is harmful to vampires, they would have to avoid taking showers, though baths might not carry the same risks. It's unclear as to whether Eli has to avoid running water, but she certainly manages to clean up nicely following the scene in which she enters Oskar's flat without an invitation and starts bleeding from her pores.

It's possible that Eli does undergo some sort of physical transformation in order to fly, but we never see it. What we do see are at least two moments when her face is fleetingly transformed into that of a much older woman. The first of these is when Oskar leads Eli into a hidden den, a sort of concrete bunker where 'some of the bigger kids hang out' and tells her, almost boastfully, how he hit back against Conny. They listen to music from the cassette player and Oskar, wanting to seal their relationship, gets out his knife and cuts his hand, proposing they mix their blood. But as soon as she smells the blood, she backs away.

Misinterpreting her reaction, Oskar says, 'It doesn't hurt'. Unable to resist the blood dripping from his hand to the ground, she crouches down and laps at it, like an animal at a waterhole. Oskar says her name, and when she looks up, she looks hundreds of years old (Eli's 'old' face belongs not to Lina Leandersson, but to an older actress, Susanne Ruben). It's a shocking moment, but so fleeting, almost subliminal, that the viewer can't be sure of what he or she has seen. Eli is showing Oskar her true face and with it her true nature, though apparently not deliberately. She orders him forcefully to go away, afraid her thirst will make her attack her new friend, but in the event, it's she who runs, straight across the estate and up a tree: we see the other side of the trunk and hear noises from her throat like those made by a cat stalking a pigeon, but we don't actually see her climb. It's from this tree that she will launch her attack on Virginia.

Blood on the floor of the 'den': Eli fleetingly shows her age

THE VAMPIRE AS SERIAL KILLER

WHY WOULD A KID KILL JOCKE?

The term 'serial killer' refers to someone who murders three or more people, one at a time, and was reportedly coined by FBI Special Agent Robert Ressler in the 1970s. The term came into vogue around the time of the release of *The Silence of the Lambs* (1991) which featured the hunt for a serial-killer called Buffalo Bill, with FBI agent Clarice Starling (Jodie Foster) seeking advice from the jailed murderer and cannibal Dr Hannibal Lecter (Anthony Hopkins).

In real life, a number of serial murderers have been called 'vampires' by the press. Peter Kürten, who was charged with nine murders and executed in 1931, was dubbed 'The Vampire of Düsseldorf'. Richard Trenton Chase, a necrophiliac who ate parts of the corpses of his victims and drank their blood, was nicknamed 'The Vampire of Sacramento'; in 1979 he stood trial on six counts of murder but took an overdose before he could go to the gas chamber. Fritz Haarmann, who in 1925 was executed for the murder of 27 boys and young men in and around Hanover (and whose killings inspired Ulli Lommel's film *The Tenderness of the Wolves* [1973]), was called both a 'vampire' and a 'werewolf'. And in 1932, an unsolved killing in Stockholm was referred to as 'the vampire murder'.

Movie vampires, who tend to leave trails of drained corpses behind them, would certainly qualify as serial killers. While many of the vampire films after the 1931 *Dracula* appear to be taking place amid all-purpose quasi-Edwardian decor, vampires began to crop up more frequently in more obviously contemporary settings in the 1970s, led by *Count Yorga, Vampire* (1970) and *Dracula AD 1972* (1972). But it was George A. Romero who first gave them a truly modern makeover, doing for vampires what he had already done for zombies with *Night of the Living Dead*, effectively updating the vampire movie from a fairy-tale set in the mythological past and relocating it in a social realist setting, just as *Let the Right One In* would do again 40 years later. *Martin* is set in a suburb of Pittsburgh (Romero went to university in Pittsburgh, and would later set many of his films in and around the state of Pennsylvania) where the industrial decay and moral confusion of the economically depressed, oil-rationed 1970s couldn't be more different from mountainous Transylviania or leafy Bray.

Martin, played by John Amplas, is a disturbed teenager who has been marginalised by his own immigrant family. He gets a job as a delivery boy and preys on the lonely housewives on his round. Martin really does believe he's a vampire and takes the clichés seriously, to the extent of kitting himself out at one point with a cloak and joke-shop fangs, though to make his victims' blood flow he resorts to slicing them with razor blades. There's nothing of the supernatural here; Martin is a pathological case, both serial killer and misunderstood teenager who is shunned, excoriated and called 'nosferatu' by his elderly cousin, who finally executes him by hammering a wooden stake through his heart. Martin is a murderer, but ironically dies when his cousin blames him for the one death in the film for which he isn't responsible: the suicide of one of the lonely housewives.

Martin's youth marks him out as a missing link between *Dracula* and later teen-orientated vampire movies such as *The Lost Boys*, which would exploit the vampire's bad-boy appeal for younger audiences but eschew the grim social realist approach for teen wish fulfilment fantasy. (*The Lost Boys* tagline was 'Sleep all day. Party all night. Never grow old. Never die. It's fun to be a vampire.') But it's arguable as to whether *Martin* is a vampire movie at all, as opposed to a pathological case study; while it's a film about a young man who *thinks* he is a vampire, there's no indication in the narrative that this is anything other than in his own imagination.

In *Martin*, however, as in *Let the Right One In*, being a vampire (even an imaginary one) is no fun at all. In fact, the vampires in both films lead a miserable existence, obliged to kill by their bloodlust and thus prevented from truly being a part of regular society. Both films demand the viewer's empathy for their vampire protagonists, without at any point presenting their murderous activities to be admirable or desirable. We are forced to reflect that, far from being the powerful, sexually attractive and glamorous creatures of many latterday vampire movies, the lives they lead are the lives of shunned outcasts - miserable, shabby and friendless.

Tony Scott's *The Hunger* (1983), adapted from Whitley Strieber's novel of the same name, is another approach to the idea of the modern vampire as serial killer, though in this the vampires lead more comfortable, almost hedonistic lives. Catherine Deneuve and David Bowie play Miriam and John, vampires who live in a Manhattan brownstone

The vampire as serial-killer (clockwise from top left): John Amplas in Martin, Bill Paxton in Near Dark, David Bowie and Catherine Deneuve in The Hunger

and prowl through New York's fashionable nightclubs in search of victims, who are lured back to the brownstone with the promise of sex before their throats are sliced open with amulets which the vampires wear around their necks.

Miriam, who has been a vampire since Egyptian times, is ageless, but John, whom she turned in the eighteenth century, has begun to age at an accelerated rate. Since he's a vampire he cannot die, but she stores his decrepit but still living body in a box in the attic alongside other boxes containing the sentient remains of her other ex-lovers, leaving her free to seek a replacement. Miriam's callousness in 'creating' companions whom she will subsequently discard like unwanted toys when they become old and ugly has an echo in Eli's abandonment of Håkan and choice of Oskar as a possible successor. But by some process which is never fully explained in the film, Miriam's initiation of John's replacement, Sarah (Susan Sarandon), goes wrong and it's Miriam who ends up a wrinkled mummylike creature in a box, while Sarah apparently inherits her fortune and role as an ageless sexual predator (the film's French title is *Les prédateurs*).

Kathryn Bigelow's *Near Dark*, a modern-day Western with vampires, is another film in which vampires behave like serial-killers. Caleb (Adrian Pasdar), an Oklahoma farmboy, is bitten on the neck by a young drifter called Mae (Jenny Wright) and is left with a thirst for blood; the vampires kidnap him in their RV and give him a week to convert to their lifestyle. He refuses to kill, though later temporarily wins their trust by helping them escape when the police raid the motel in which they're holed up.

Unlike Martin or Eli, the vampires of *Near Dark* are not solitary creatures; they have formed themselves into an alternative 'family', a clan degenerate enough to rival the cannibal rubes of *The Texas Chainsaw Massacre* (1974), though probably cleverer and certainly better travelled. 'Mother' and 'father' are Diamondback (Jenette Goldstein) and Jesse (Lance Henriksen); Severen (Bill Paxton) plays the role of the delinquent older son, Mae the daughter and Homer (Joshua Miller) the youngest, though since he's a vampire he's much older than he looks. They travel around in goods trains or stolen cars or camper vans (obliterating their tracks by burning their cast-offs), covering the windows of their vehicles with light-tight cooking foil (rolls of which they keep handy for this very purpose) and hunkering down in bundles of blankets to protect them from the light when travelling by day. They bunk in empty barns or cheap motels, feed on motorists and hitchhikers, or drop in at remote roadside bars to drink the blood of the redneck (literally, once our nomads have finished with them) clientele. These vampires don't have fangs; they use flick knives or razor-sharp spurs to slice their victims' throats, though they don't even need those weapons, to judge by the way Severen is able to kill one man simply by crushing his head. If Martin and Eli have been marginalised against their will, these vampire-travellers have deliberately severed all links to polite society, the only social element they have left being their parody of the family unit. They're white trash, the underclass, ultimate outsiders who, despite their non-luxurious lifestyle, seem to take a perverse pleasure from operating beyond the boundaries of normal behaviour. But they are not lone operators; they still need each other.

In *Martin* and *Near Dark*, apart from the blood drinking and (in *Near Dark*'s case) longevity and superior strength, these 'vampires' could almost be interchangeable with human serial-killers. Indeed, Eli and Håkan are classic serial killers, moving from place to place, leaving a trail of unsolved murders behind them. In the course of the film, Håkan succeeds in killing only the youth in the park, though he goes about it so methodically (albeit ineptly) and without apparent moral qualm that we naturally assume he has killed before. He is ready to kill again, and gets as far as stringing up the youth in the changing-rooms of the gymnasium, but his clumsiness, ineptitude and a sort of fatalistic resignation (he already senses that Eli has found someone to replace him) get the better of him and he gives up.

Eli, on the other hand, claims seven victims. The deaths of Håkan and Virginia are indirect and might be viewed, at least partially, as suicides, and that of Lacke could possibly be regarded as legitimate self-defence, but this leaves at least four cold-blooded murders. She kills Jocke for his blood, but the deaths of Conny, Martin and Jimmy are swift, merciless and vengeful; she could have let them off with a severe beating, but instead she decapitates and mutilates them.

We don't know anything about Jocke beyond the fact that he's one of Lacke's drinking companions and is ready to help a child in distress. Eli is hiding in the shadow of the underpass, saying 'Help me'. Jocke approaches her to see if he can help, but his Good Samaritan gesture is rewarded by Eli jumping on him and sinking her teeth into his neck. It's a method of entrapment similar to that practised by *Near Dark*'s Homer, who lies on the road, pretending to have fallen off his bike, until a passing motorist stops and bends over him to see if he's hurt.

'Help me.' Eli and Jocke in the underpass

The assault itself is not like the traditional vampire attack, where the vampire (usually male) is taller than his victim (usually female) and bends over her neck. The earliest cinema vampire attacks were suggested rather than shown, with the victim shrinking back as Schreck or Lugosi approaches slowly before stooping over them, sometimes enveloping them in his cloak as he does so. Even Lee as Dracula, though often seen hovering directly over jugulars and with blood on or around his mouth, was never shown actually biting into flesh. But as censorship loosened and special effects became more realistic, the vampire killings became faster and messier until, in *Vamp*, Katrina is shown tearing into her victim's neck with her fangs.

Nowadays, in films like *30 Days of Night*, the vampires move so rapidly the effect is often conveyed via jump cuts. Eli moves fast, too, but filmed in long shot and without the help of modern film-making gimmickry. Due to her small size, she can't stoop over her victims unless they're lying down and, unlike vampires with an adult appearance, she's not physically equipped to seduce her victim sexually, but uses her childlike appearance as a lure and turns her victim's best intentions against them by pretending to be helpless and crying for help. Perhaps, also, her lack of sustenance has so weakened her she needs to trick her victim into coming to *her*, after which her modus operandi is to leap on to them and wrap her legs around their waste, putting her in a position to batten on to their necks. The result is a horrible parody of the way adults carry small children held against their bodies, a role reversal with the child placed in a position of power against the adult.

As with the murder in the park, Eli's attack is filmed mostly in long shot, distancing the viewer. It's accompanied by a low animal roar, followed by lots of horrible sucking noises on the soundtrack. Afterwards, Eli methodically easily breaks Jocke's neck, which seems brutal, even unnecessary – surely, we think, if she let him alone, he would recover? But, as we will see later, after the attack on Virginia, it's an act of mercy. Afterwards she slumps forward on to the corpse in a parody of post-coital fatigue, letting out a sob, her physical actions expressing tiredness and, perhaps, remorse and disgust, even as her painful need for blood has finally been assuaged. As Alfredson points out, 'She's really, really tired'. How many times has she done this? Unlike Håkan, whose bungling we have already seen, her method is quick and efficient, presumably perfected throughout centuries of practice (though it's still pretty messy, leaving her face and clothes covered in blood). But the fact that she has arranged for Håkan to collect blood on her behalf suggests she would rather not have to do it at all.

This is far from the libidinous bloodsucking of the traditional vampire. Eli's method is not so much sexual as parasitical, like that of a demonic child attacking its parent, or ivy clinging to its host plant. But viewed objectively, it's sloppy behaviour; whereas Håkan travelled a couple of metro stops away to kill the youth in the park, Eli's thirst has led her to kill in what is essentially her own backyard, and in a spot overlooked by dozens of windows.

This time it's Håkan's turn to yell at Eli. In a two-shot depicting Oskar's and Eli's adjacent windows, we hear him noisily berating Eli, presumably for what she has just done, though his words are inaudible, both to us and to Oskar, who listens through the wall, stroking at it longingly with his hand, still desperate to make a connection. It's the first indication we've had that Håkan is not entirely subservient to Eli, that there are rules to their relationship and she has just broken one, and that he's not so cowed by her that he will not give her ticking off. Once again, they're behaving like an old married couple; forced to stay together, and nagging and bickering when not taking each other for granted. Though Eli apparently has the upper hand due to Håkan's almost slavelike devotion, she is still dependant on him – and she needs him now. He emerges from the building, preparing to clean up the mess that Eli has left behind. The fact that she's left fewer clues than Håkan did in the park is offset by her lack of prudence.

And, unknown by her, there *was* a witness, who *will* later enable Lacke to connect Eli to the murder and almost prove her undoing. Gösta, the cat man, has seen the attack from his window and not long afterwards enters the Sun Palace to tell the others what he has just seen. They follow him out to where Jocke was killed. 'I was out on the balcony and I saw Jocke and this kid,' he says. But the corpse has already disappeared, leaving a bloodstain buried in the snow.

But this is not a fantasy in which corpses conveniently vanish by themselves. (Joss Whedon and his colleagues consciously made the decision that in the TV series *Buffy the Vampire Slayer* the corpses of any vampires slain by Buffy should disappear: 'I didn't think it would be fun to have fifteen minutes of "Let's Clean up the Bodies" each time' (DVD commentary, *Buffy the Vampire Slayer* Season 1, Episode 1: *Welcome to the Hellmouth*,

20th Century Fox). At this very moment, Håkan is laboriously dragging a child's red plastic sled laden with Jocke's corpse towards the frozen lake. In this scene, Lindqvist says, they were trying, '...to give an idea of the difficulty and the tediousness and all the work and the weight... involved in killing and disposing of people'. The lengthy, arduous process of getting rid of the murder victim has many a precedent in horror films and thrillers, and often has the result of making the viewer empathise, however reluctantly, with the killer. The most famous example is that of Norman Bates in *Psycho*, disposing of the corpse of Marion Crane after his 'mother' has murdered her in the shower; we in the audience, still shocked by the abrupt removal of our principal identification figure, find ourselves transferring our emotional investment to the only alternative at hand – Norman – as he puts Crane's corpse in her car and sinks it in the swamp. For a moment, the car looks as though it won't sink, and we find ourselves willing it to go under. All of a sudden, we're emotional accessories to the murder.

Håkan tips the corpse into the water around a waste-pipe, the only part of the lake where the water isn't frozen, and pokes it under with a long red metal rod he finds. This is the very same metal rod which will later be found and used as an impromptu weapon by Oskar when he fights back against the bullies. Håkan is unwittingly passing the baton to his successor.

Håkan's next attempt to collect blood for Eli is even more of a disaster than the debacle in the park, and he seems to know in advance that it will end badly; this time, he packs a bottle of acid into his murder kit and tells Eli, 'There are people who know my face, who know that I live here with you'. Presumably he's referring to Lacke and his friends at the Sun Palace. He's prepared to inflict terrible damage on himself for Eli; what will she do for him in return? Sounding like a jealous housewife (much like Humbert Humbert nagging Lolita when she's late coming home from school) he asks, 'Could you not see that boy tonight?' Eli, who's looking hungry again, strokes his face tenderly, perhaps regretfully, but doesn't reply. Like a wife who knows her husband is about to be unfaithful with a younger, prettier woman, or perhaps like an employee who senses he is about to be made redundant, Håkan looks resigned.

Håkan's botched assault on the youth at the gym is filmed in a sort of visual shorthand, requiring us to fill in the gaps with what we know of his modus operandi from having already seen the murder in the park. One minute Håkan is peering in through the window at some youths playing a ball game in the gym. The next, his victim is strung upside-down from some coathooks in a changing-room, with Håkan already dressed in the plastic mac, his murder-wear. But this time, just as he's getting ready to slit the boy's throat, the lights go out. And then, while he's fiddling with a torch, the youth's friends come looking for him, and the victim regains consciousness and begins to struggle and yell. Instead of fleeing, Håkan retreats into the shower room with the jar of acid, says 'Eli' and deliberately pours the acid over his face.

The divided frame: Håkan and the acid, his victim rescued by friends

In contrast to his actions, the piano music on the soundtrack is delicate and poignant. The piano music continues over a shot of Eli's back. She's sitting on Håkan's bedding, facing the wall. At first it looks as though she's reacting telepathically to Håkan's predicament, or even missing him, but then she raises a hand to the wall. It's not Håkan she's thinking of, but Oskar in the flat next door – another of the film's sly little ways of linking Håkan and Oskar in our subconscious.

An entire day passes, as days tend to pass in *Let the Right One In*, with brief scenes of Oskar lifting weights, finding his trousers soaked in a urinal in the changing room (those bullies again), and setting off for home, through the snow, legs bare in his gym shorts, carrying his sodden trousers in a plastic bag. And bingo! It's night-time again.

The radio in Eli's flat announces, 'An unidentified man was arrested yesterday, charged with murder'. She's still lying on Håkan's bed (though since a day has passed, one assumes she has slept in a light-tight part of the flat), her back to the camera, touching the wall gently with her fingers. When she hears the newsreader mention 'self-inflicted facial wounds,' she knows instantly what has happened, and gets up.

There's a cut to the reception area of the hospital. Offscreen, a voice says, 'Come on in, through those doors'. Eli, feet bare, pads into the empty reception area and says to the receptionist, 'Excuse me, I'm looking for my dad'. Here we get another glimpse of Eli the manipulator, exploiting her little girl persona, and dumbing down for the benefit of the adult who may be able to provide her with the information she needs. The ploy works; the hospital receptionist tells her Håkan is on the seventh floor, under police guard. In fact, the play for sympathy works *too* well, since the receptionist says, 'Oh, you poor thing,' and hurries after Eli after she leaves. We see the receptionist standing in front of the hospital building in long shot, looking around for the poor little girl who has vanished; when she gives up and goes back inside, we notice a dark shape detache itself from the shadows on the building in the background and scurry upwards over the façade. Eli has been hiding in plain sight, but it's only when she moves that we spot her.

Eli is on the window ledge, outside the room, unable to enter without an invitation. But Håkan is no longer in any position to extend one; the acid has destroyed his larynx. (But hasn't she already been invited into the hospital? Perhaps the vampire needs a separate invitation for each threshold she crosses.) Håkan, on a respirator, goes over to the window and shows her his ruined face. Perhaps there is pity in her response, but in truth it's hard to tell; it might just be what we want to see in accordance with the Kuleshov effect, in which, in the spectator's eyes, a man's neutral expression takes on various different meanings depending on its juxtaposition with shots of a bowl of soup, a girl or a coffin.

Håkan's ruined face; the nearest thing to a shock-horror moment

Håkan unplugs his respirator and offers Eli his neck, at the same time showing us what remains of the right side of his face: it's a mass of ruined flesh, exposed teeth and tendons with half-melted features, like an anatomy model. It's probably the nearest thing in the film to a shock-horror moment, except the effect is more pitiable than horrific, with sad, minimalist music once again countering the gruesome imagery. It's all over for Håkan, and from what little we've seen of his life, it hasn't been a happy one. Where did it all go wrong? Now he's making the ultimate sacrifice, offering his own blood to the vampire in place of the nourishment he has conspicuously failed to collect by other means. When Eli has had her fill, she simply lets him tumble out of the window. There's blood on her mouth. She seems contemplative for a moment, then turns and disappears out of frame. We hear the sound of what could be giant wings flapping.

THE VAMPIRE AS METAPHOR

Horror stories have always dabbled in those parts of the human condition that more respectable mainstream culture dares not touch. Vampire movies and books provide an indirect way of dealing with the sort of subjects that are still regarded in certain quarters as taboo, or as too embarrassing or intense or upsetting to discuss outside the safe haven of a psychiatrist's office; subjects like sex, death, intimacy and big, messy emotions which can end up seeming mawkish or banal if tackled head-on. It's a way of sneaking the unmentionable out of the quarantine of restrained good taste, and into the public domain, though it's generally the subconscious rather than the intellect which latches on to it there.

The subtext of the vampire has changed over the years according to the social and sexual mores, political situations, religious beliefs and fashions of the day. Lugosi and Lee might once have recoiled before the trappings of Christianity – crucifixes, holy water and wafers – but the potency of such symbols has faded, though crucifixes are still displayed, as much for superstitious reasons or as fashion accessories (cf early Madonna videos) as religious symbols. There are echoes, in the way Håkan suspends his victims upside-down to drain them of their blood, in the resurrection of Dracula in Hammer's *Dracula, Prince of Darkness* (1966), where an unlucky victim is hung upside-down by Dracula's servant and his throat cut so the blood spilled over Dracula's ashes in a scene which appears to be a deliberate perversion of the crucifixion. And the idea of drinking blood has echoes of the Eucharist, as shown explicity in Park Chan-Wook's *Thirst* (2009), a loose adaptation of Émile Zola's novel *Thérèse Raquin* (1867), in which one of the adulterous vampire lovers is a priest.

Eli's very name is loaded with religious significance. It's the name of an Old Testament prophet and a common boy's name in Hebrew cultures, but also sounds like the more feminine 'Elly' as well as the acronym E.L.E. (Extinction Level Event) as featured, for example, in the sci-fi disaster movie *Deep Impact* (1998), in which a reporter investigating a politician's resignation assumes the 'Ellie' she keeps hearing about is the name of his mistress. According to the gospels of Matthew and Mark, Jesus cried, 'Eli Eli lema sabachthani?' ('My God, My God, why hast thou forsaken me?') at the ninth hour of his crucifixion (the same words are also spoken by David in the Book of Psalms) which casts Håkan's last word ('Eli') in a very different light, making the act of pouring the acid over his face seem almost like a religious offering. (The investigating detectives in the novel come to this very same conclusion.)

Does Håkan regard Eli as some sort of deity? Certainly, she is gifted with such godlike superpowers as longevity and super-strength, but she also rules Håkan's life to such an extent she's virtually playing the role of a god, demanding regular blood sacrifices in which Håkan acts as a sort of high priest. According to the novel, she 'saved' him from destitution and alcoholism, enlisting him much as Jesus enlisted his disciples. And, again in the novel, witnesses to the swimming-pool massacre maintain that Oskar 'had been rescued by an angel' – albeit an angel which had ripped the heads off two of its victims. But in most other respects, *Let the Right One In* is a secular vampire movie; we see no churches or priests, and no-one tries to protect themselves against the vampire by brandishing crucifixes or holy water.

So what is the vampirism a metaphor for in *Let the Right One In*? In early Hollywood, aggressive sexuality was often depicted as the province of unAmerican foreigners; Theodosia Goodman, a tailor's daughter from Ohio, was made over as silent star Theda Bara (an anagram for 'arab death') who starred as a 'vamp' in *A Fool There Was* (1915) and was given a fabricated history in which she was said to be the offspring of an artist and an Arabian princess. Lugosi, in Tod Browning's *Dracula*, represented menacing masculinity with his heavy Hungarian accent and heavy-browed stare. As Hammer's Dracula, Christopher Lee unleashed the libidos of prim Victorian matrons under the very noses of their menfolk. The sexuality in Hammer films became increasingly explicit as censorship relaxed during the 1960s, with décolletage becoming progressively lower as vampires zeroed in on the heaving bosoms of their female victims. In *The Hunger*, *Vamp* and *Near Dark*, the biting and bloodsucking are incorporated into heavy petting, or the sex act itself, with penetration of the flesh triggering an almost orgasmic reaction.

Yet sexuality is conspicuous by its absence in *Let the Right One In*. Oskar and Eli share a bed, hug and kiss, but their relationship is entirely innocent – or as innocent as any relationship can be when one of the protagonists is hundreds of years older than the other. She (or the little boy she started out as) was transformed into a vampire before she reached puberty, and her interest in Oskar seems to be as companion and soulmate rather than as an object of lust; her sexual awakening apparently never developed beyond that of her physical age.

This is in contrast to Claudia in Anne Rice's *Interview with the Vampire*, (filmed in 1994 by Neil Jordan, where she is played by Kirsten Dunst). Claudia is the only substantial female character in a story which is otherwise remarkable for its homoeroticism. The anti-hero Lestat turns her into a vampire in a bid to keep Louis by his side, thus making of her the ultimate fag hag – a prepubescent girl who will never do anything as vulgar as grow breasts or hips, perhaps casting Lestat and Louis as the vampire equivalents of those fashion designers whose preferred models are skinny girls who look more like adolescent boys than grown women. Claudia, fated 'to be the demon child forever' (*Interview with the Vampire*, Anne Rice, 1976/Ballantine, 2009, p101), is just five years old when Lestat turns her into a vampire; as the decades pass, she continues to have the body of a five-year-old while her intellect and sexuality mature into that of an adult, and begins to resent the fact that she will never physically develop into a mature woman; the incongruence seems to drive her insane: 'Yet more and more her doll-like face seemed to possess two totally aware adult eyes, and innocence seemed lost somewhere with neglected toys and the loss of a certain patience' (p102). Claudia, unlike Eli, is not innocent; she gets a sadistic pleasure from toying with her victims before killling them.

Fated to be the demon child forever: Kirsten Dunst in Interview with the Vampire

In *Near Dark*, the child vampire Homer (Joshua Miller) asks, 'Have you any idea what it's like to be a big man on the inside and have a small body on the outside?'. He introduces himself with the distinctly unchildlike gambit of aggressively grabbing Caleb's groin and spelling his name: 'Mispronounce it and I wouldn't want to be you.' Even with an awareness of his true age, it's still faintly shocking to see him smoking as he plays 'Five-Card Russian Roulette' with his fellow vampires. But Homer, despite having his surrogate family around him, yearns for a soulmate; once he's met Caleb's younger sister Sarah, all he can think of is turning her into a vampire to replace Mae, who has rejected him for Caleb: 'I turned Mae,' he says bitterly to Caleb, 'then she went off and turned you'. In other words, Homer looked on his relationship with Mae, prior to Caleb's arrival, as a relationship between equals, while she, one imagines, did not.

Oskar, having concluded Eli is a vampire, asks if she's old, to which she replies, 'I'm 12. But I've been 12 for a long time'. Perhaps she really is still 12, as opposed to an older individual merely posing as a 12-year-old. In any case, that two 12-year-olds, one of them naked, can be shown in bed together, being affectionate towards one another, but without a trace of prurience, is one of the most impressive balancing acts in *Let the Right One In*. The scene follows directly on from Eli's visit to the hospital where she has just 'assisted' in Håkan's suicide. She taps at Oskar's window and asks, 'Can I come in?' Oskar wakes drowsily, and she tells him not to look at her, 'But you have to say that I can come in'.

Once invited, she tells him to close his eyes, slips out of her clothes and climbs naked into his bed to lie behind him. Now wide awake, he asks, 'How did you get in?' She tells him she flew, and he replies, 'Yeah, sure', before realising she's not wearing anything. She plays a guessing game ('Higgledy piggledy shout. How many fingers are out?'). He asks her if she wants to go steady, then, when she requests clarification, asks her to be his girlfriend.

'Oskar,' she says, 'I'm not a girl' – to which he replies (in a response reminiscent of Joe E Brown's 'Nobody's perfect' at the end of *Some Like It Hot* [1959]) 'But do you want to go steady or not?' Only after she's established through questioning that 'going steady' doesn't involve behaving any differently from the way they're behaving now, does Eli accept the offer ('Then we'll go steady'). 'It'll be you and me', she says. Oskar is delighted. He goes back to sleep as she strokes his arm.

This entire sequence is extraordinary – two pre-teens in bed together, one of them naked and with blood on her face. In striking contrast to the long and medium shots of the murder scenes, it's filmed mostly in intimate close-up, in semi-darkness. There's no hint of prurience or sexual content, but neither is there an impression of forced abstinence, as in *Twilight*. Both Oskar and Eli are sexually innocent, but longing for emotional intimacy and companionship.

SEX AND THE VAMPIRE

I'M NOT A GIRL.

'What if I'm not the hero? What if I'm the bad guy?' asks Edward Cullen, the brooding vampire boyfriend in *Twilight*, played by British actor Robert Pattinson in the film version of Stephenie Meyer's bestselling supernatural romance for young adults. Edward needn't worry; he's no bloodsucking fiend. Vampires may originally have struck fear into the hearts of East European peasants as the ghastly walking cadavers of Carpathian myth; Lugosi or Lee may have violated the throats of their female victims in a form of supernatural rape, but by the end of the first decade of the twenty-first century, it was women who were calling the shots. Instead of screaming and getting bitten and turned into passive playthings, they were reaching out to their erstwhile ravishers and – horror of horrors – having relationships with them.

In the 1960s, while Hammer's vampires were still bloodsucking bad guys, lovelorn 175-year-old Barnabas Collins was already attracting a cult following on his TV soap opera *Dark Shadows* (1966-71). Then in 1976, Anne Rice played up the romantic Byronic aspects of the myth in the first of her Vampire Chronicles, *Interview with the Vampire*; but it was still largely a guy, if not a gay, thing. Two years later, Chelsea Quinn Yarbro's *Hotel Transylvania* (1978) launched an historical adventure series featuring the undead Count Saint-Germain, who later turns at least two female lovers into vampires with their own spin-off novels.

Fright Night, while not altogether straightfaced, is not a spoof but a vampire version of the Boy Who Cried Wolf. Charley, the young hero, suspects that his new next-door neighbour is a vampire, but instead of befriending him, as Oskar does with Eli in *Light the Right One In*, he denounces and ultimately helps to destroy him. Like *The Lost Boys*, released two years later, *Fright Night* was aimed at teenage filmgoers, but co-stars veteran actor Roddy McDowall as the has-been host of a TV horror show, to whom the young hero turns for help. Both *The Lost Boys* and *Fright Night* have thinly veiled homoerotic undertones; in each case the token girlfriend seems like a 'beard', whose role it is to flag the male characters' heterosexuality, since the central 'relationship' in each film is the one between the young hero and the male vampire(s).

Francis Coppola's *Bram Stoker's Dracula* restored the heterosexuality, but made the vampire (Gary Oldman as Dracula) into even more of a lovelorn romantic figure. James V. Hart's screenplay shows the Count's origins in the historical character of Vlad III, Prince of Wallachia, popularly known as Vlad the Impaler, the fifteenth century despot later hailed by Romanians as a national hero for his part in the struggle against the Turks. The character of Vlad is one of the generally accepted inspirations for the modern vampire myth (along with the fifteenth century childkiller Gilles de Rais, Elizabeth Báthory, and Lord Byron) and Hart's screenplay picks up on a little-known detail of his story – that of his first wife, who committed suicide – and suggests his original transformation into a vampire came about after he cursed God after her death.

Thus, Dracula as played by Oldman, while dangerous, is no implacably evil villain, but a romantic anti-hero who is drawn towards Mina because of her resemblance to his long-lost love. (Coppola's film, incidentally, shares several key plot elements with *Dracula Exotica* aka *Love at First Gulp* [1980], one of two 'adult' vampire movies starring Jamie Gillis as Dracula.) Though his transformations into rats and wolves, and his murderous blood-drinking are still monstrous, Dracula's lovesickness and the visual stylisation (especially Eiko Ishioka's elaborate costume designs) make the film seem more decadent romance than horror movie. In any case, despite all the blood sloshing around, and like the vampire films that would soon follow, it was a curiously toothless vampire tale, and not remotely frightening. The vampire was beginning to lose his bite. In symbolic terms, he was being systematically defanged, emasculated, pussy-whipped into service as a boy band pin-up whose mad, bad and dangerous reputation as a vampire can't disguise his essential squeaky-clean wholesomeness.

But it wasn't until 1997 – when Joss Whedon, unhappy with the 1992 film made from his original screenplay of *Buffy the Vampire Slayer*, turned the concept into a seven-season TV phenomenon – that girlpower really got into its stride. It wasn't just the cute blonde cheerleader's proactive vampire-slaying that made her so influential; it was her relationships with two of the vampires, Angel and Spike. The series played with and rang variations on a full complement of metaphors, including the agonies of adolescent love, the terrors of high school and the difficulties of finding one's place in the world, transgressive sex, forced abstinence, viruses, physical transformation and personality change.

Buffy the Vampire Slayer: *Sarah Michelle Gellar in the TV show*

And in the wake of Buffy and Lauren K Hamilton's series of novels about another vampire hunter, Anita Blake (launched in 1993 with *Guilty Pleasures*), came a flood of fang-fiction aimed at a female readership eager to find worthy successors to Heathcliff, Mr Rochester and Darcy, the Byronic hero who is not just mad, bad and dangerous to know, but irresistible to the female reader. The worldwide success of Stephenie Meyer's *Twilight*, the most popular of these paranormal romances, indicates that Edward Cullen is what generations of young (and maybe not so young) women have been waiting for; though, despite Edward's century of existence, it seems he has yet to develop a personality. As Bella, the lovestruck narrator, describes him in the books, 'He had the most beautiful soul, more beautiful than his brilliant mind or his incomparable face or his glorious body,' though she never elaborates beyond that.

The first *Twilight* film sticks to the winning formula of Meyer's novel; 17-year-old Bella moves in with her divorced dad, sheriff of a small town in overcast Washington State, and enrols at a new school where she notices a clique of extra-pale pupils who don't eat lunch. (The question of why vampires who have lived for more than 100 years would need to attend school in the first place is never addressed; if the idea is to maintain a regular human facade, surely it would arouse suspicion when Edward and his siblings failed to grow older like their classmates, or turned up for their first-year biology class for the twentieth time.) Edward belongs to a coven of vampires who, like the nomadic travellers of *Near Dark*, have formed themselves into an alternative 'family'. But the members of Edward's family, unlike the *Near Dark* vampires, are actively trying to blend into human society. They drink the blood of animals rather than people and Carlisle Cullen, the patriarch, works as a doctor at the local hospital.

Meyer's one big twist on traditional vampire lore is having her vampires avoid sunlight not because it destroys them, but because it makes them glitter, hence the Cullens' choice of the relatively sun-free Pacific North-West as home – though you do wonder how Carlisle would explain his absence from the hospital if ever there happened to be a medical emergency on a sunny day.

Bella and Edward fall in love, but their relationship never gets beyond first base – kissing, chin-holding, declarations of eternal love – because he's tempted by the smell of her blood and is frightened of losing control. *Time* magazine dubbed it 'the erotics of abstinence' ('Stephenie Meyer: A New JK Rowling?' Lev Grossman, *Time*, 24 April, 2008). The relationship between Bella and Edward, like that between Oskar and Eli, is fundamentally a little creepy, since despite his youthful looks he's actually her senior by some eighty years, making their liaison the vampire quivalent of a paedophile posing as a teenager in an internet chatroom. The difference, though, is that Edward was already a young man when he died, whereas Eli appears trapped in an eternal pre-pubescence.

'What if I'm the bad guy?' Robert Pattinson as the brooding vampire boyfriend in the Twilight saga

Vampirism is often presented as a metaphor for 'forbidden' sexuality. Dracula drinks most often (but not exclusively) from women, his attentions stirring their repressed libidos, but anticipating Stoker's novel by some 25 years is Sheridan Le Fanu's novella *Carmilla* (1872) in which the female vampire preys only on other women. The story, which is set in Styria (a state in the south-east of present-day Austria), is narrated by 19-year-old Laura, who tells of her friendship with Carmilla (or Mircalla, as she is sometimes known) Karnstein, who comes to stay with Laura's family after a coach accident. The newcomer, who doesn't get up until the afternoon and who can't stand the sound of hymn-singing, quickly becomes intimate with Laura:

> It was like the ardour of a lover; it embarrassed me; it was hateful and yet overpowering; and with gloating eyes she drew me to her, and her hot lips travelled

along my cheek in kisses; and she would whisper, almost in sobs, "You are mine, you shall be mine, and you and I are one for ever". (*In a Glass Darkly*, Sheridan Le Fanu, 1872/Oxford 1993, p264)

Laura dreams of being bitten on the breast by a large catlike creature which changes into a female figure before vanishing. She weakens and falls ill, but she and her father meet up with General Spielsdorf, whose daughter died after befriending a mysterious stranger; with the help of the descendant of a vampire-hunting hero, they locate Carmilla's hidden tomb and destroy her.

In films, female vampires have long carried connotations of lesbianism. *Dracula's Daughter* (1936) picks up where Todd Browning's *Dracula* ends, with the Count's remains stolen by his daughter, the Countess Marya Zaleska (Gloria Holden) who is desperate to shake off the vampire urges she has inherited from her father. When the destruction of his remains fails to cure her, she seeks help from a psychologist who remarks, 'You know, this is the first woman's flat I've been in that didn't have at least 20 mirrors in it'. The Countess and her assistant Sandor search for young women to pose as artist's models, but instead of painting them she drinks their blood.

The vampiric act in itself is usually perceived as aggressive and masculine since it involves penetration (fangs puncturing skin). The male vampire is drawn, as if by sexual desire, towards his chosen victim, but instead of having sex with her, he sucks her blood (and the act of sucking, with its oral connotations, carries an added sexual charge). Traditionally, the only legitimate sex is that of a heterosexual couple, preferably with the male partner taking the dominant role. By this reasoning, therefore, there has to be something particularly unnatural about the female vampire, who has assumed the masculine role. So it's little wonder she is so often perceived as a lesbian.

Hammer's 'Karnstein Trilogy' was loosely inspired by Le Fanu's story; *The Vampire Lovers* (1970), in which Ingrid Pitt played Marcilla/Mircalla/Carmilla Karnstein, had a plot loosely based on the novella; *Lust for a Vampire* (1971) featured Mircalla/Carmilla Karnstein infiltrating a girls' finishing school, though she also seduces the headmaster; while *Twins of Evil* (1971) also features members of the Karnstein family.

Daughters of Darkness illustrates the way vampire movies can play fast and loose with gender roles and sexuality. The young honeymoon couple, Stefan (John Karlen) and Valerie (Danielle Ouimet), begin by declaring, perversely, that they *don't* love each other, as if this were the most normal thing in the world. They arrive by train at an out-of-season hotel in Ostend, ostensibly to get the cross-channel ferry, but Stefan seems reluctant to introduce his new bride to his mother in England, to whom he talks on the telephone. When we finally see 'mother' at the other end of the phone, she turns out to be a middle-aged man (Dutch film-maker Fons Radermakers) in florid make-up. While he/she plays no direct role in the narrative which unfolds (the couple never leave Belgium) her presence casts ambiguity on the sexuality and certainly the fidelity of Stefan, who turns out to be a sadist and a voyeur; he whips his wife with a belt, ogles the corpse of a murder victim and apparently has no scruples in trying to have sex with Ilona, the attractive young 'secretary' of another of the hotel's guests, the Countess Báthory. As the hotel's concierge points out, the Countess (played by French art-house diva Delphine Seyrig) bears a remarkable resemblance to her ancestor, whom he saw as a small boy. But she is, of course, one and the same; a peripetetic 300-year-old vampire.

Kümel's film spins some interesting new twists on vampire clichés: playing on the traditional vampire's aversion to running water, the Countess and her protegée are unwilling or unable to go outside when it's raining. Stefan tries playfully to drag Ilona under the shower, where the running water throws her into a violent panic, resulting in her accidental death. Meanwhile, in nearby Bruges, young women are found with their throats cut. Seyrig is, in fact, leading the life of an unusually soignée serial killer, drifting from place to place, fang-free but impeccably lipsticked, tightly coiffed à la Dietrich and clad in chic-est red chiffon or silver sequin-studded gowns.

With the death of Ilona, the vampire's assistant (and, it is suggested, her lesbian lover), the Countess must find a replacement; she already has her eye on Valerie. The substitution of one helpmate for another will later be echoed in *The Hunger* and *Let the Right One In*, while the ending of *The Hunger* is very close to that of *Daughters of Darkness*; the Countess is apparently destroyed in a car crash which impales her on the branch of a tree as the wreckage goes up in flames, but in a coda we see Valerie, now speaking with the Countess's voice, in the company of a young couple, having presumably taken over the vampire's role of seductive predator so that the entire murderous cycle can begin again.

Daughters of Darkness: *playing fast and loose with gender roles*

In *Let the Right One In*, there are hints, with Eli's repeated protestations of 'I'm not a girl', and an almost subliminal glimpse of her scarred pubic area, that she is indeed not a girl, but a castrated boy (this is made explicit in the novel, where her origins and castration are described in detail) but all this serves to suggest not so much that the relationship is a homoerotic one, as that precise gender definitions are irrelevant. Oskar, with his puny physique, platinum blond hair and delicate colouring, is more girlish than Eli, but both characters are defined by their prepubescence, with their interplay remaining innocent and asexual, though – as children's friendships often do – it mimics the format of a relationship between older teenagers when Oskar asks Eli to 'go steady' with him.

BECOMING A VAMPIRE

I DON'T WANT TO LIVE.

As the Zeitgeist changed along with the moral climate, vampire movies became a metaphor for drug addiction in films like *Martin*, *Near Dark* and Abel Ferrara's *The Addiction* (1995) in which Lili Taylor plays a New York philosophy student who is bitten by a vampire, starts spouting even more psychobabble than before ('Existence is the search for relief from our habit, and our habit is the only relief we can find') and turns her own graduation party into a bloodsucking orgy. After a couple of decades of more or less unfettered sexual liberation, Aids hit the headlines in the 1980s and sex was once again regarded as a dangerous pursuit. The vampire life-and-death cycle offered a convenient way of dramatising the idea of a virus transmissable through body fluids, leading, in some cases, to extreme physical changes and, often, death. The first sound in *Near Dark* is of an insect hum, and the first image an extreme close-up of a mosquito drawing blood from human skin, while Caleb and Mae's vampirism is finally cured, rather miraculously, with blood transfusions (which had their precedent in Stoker's novel). *Bram Stoker's Dracula* played up the Aids angle with close-ups of slide projections of swarming bacilli.

When Virginia is bitten in *Let the Right One In*, she says to Lacke, 'That kid, she must have infected me somehow'. And it does indeed look as though she's in the grip of a particularly unpleasant virus, one that makes her unable to consume normal food and allergic to sunlight, and gives her a craving for blood.

'What would it be like when you were starting to turn into a vampire?' asks Lindqvist. 'Before you were a fully-fledged vampire, knowing how to do everything?'

The first and probably best known transformation of human into vampire is that of Lucy Westenra in Stoker's *Dracula*. Lucy is visited night after night by the Count, who drains her blood until she sickens and dies. A week after her death, Van Helsing and Dr Seward open her coffin to find her, as Dr Seward reports, 'more radiantly beautiful than ever; and I could not believe that she was dead. The lips were red, nay redder than before; and on the cheeks was a delicate bloom'.

In *The Hunger*, Sarah, a doctor who has been investigating the ageing process, is turned by Miriam, who is on the lookout for a mate after the physical decline of her former companion, John. Miriam gets Sarah drunk and hypnotises her into bed to the strains of the 'Flower Duet' from Léo Delibes' opera *Lakmé*. In a dreamlike lesbian romp, they exchange fluids by sucking the blood from each other's arms. Afterwards, Sarah is unable to stomach solid food, and vomits into the lavatory like a heroin addict. One of her colleagues takes a blood test and, upon discovering her blood has been infected with another strain, orders Sarah to roll up her sleeves, as though expecting to see needle marks. And she is indeed behaving like a drug addict in the throes of withdrawal: perspiring and (like Eli) suffering from painful stomach cramps. A passer-by calls her a 'crazy fucking junkie'. At first Sarah manages to resist her vampire urges, but finally, driven by thirst, she kills her boyfriend and drinks his blood.

Miriam maps out her future: 'You will sleep six hours in every twenty-four. You will feed one day in seven. And from this moment you will never grow old. Not a minute. You'll be young forever.' As we already know, she is lying, and in her careful choice of words, she does indeed hint that eternal life is perhaps not all it's cracked up to be: 'You're damned to live forever. There's no release, no end. And I need you to share it with me. After a while you will forget what you were. Then you'll begin to love me, as I love you. Forever. Forever and ever.' Note the words, 'I need you to share it with me'. Me, me, me: Miriam's actions are purely selfish; she's fending off her own solitude without a thought for her companion's eventual fate – unlike Eli, whose murderous attack at the end of *Let the Right One In* seems more to stem from a genuine desire to protect her friend, Oskar, than to enlist him as a companion.

The human-to-vampire transformation is also depicted in detail in *Frostbiten*, though here it's mostly played for laughs. Sebastian (who has taken an experimental vaccine in the belief it's a recreational drug) also suffers from painful stomach cramps. He vomits bile and is unable to assuage his thirst by drinking water, milk, even tomato ketchup. The timing couldn't be worse; he is due at his girlfriend's family house for dinner. (There's a similar play on the horror-comedy of social embarrassment in *Drag Me To Hell* [2009], in which the heroine's dinner with her fiancé's parents is blighted by hallucinations caused by a gypsy's curse.) In an accumulation of comic detail, his girlfriend's father turns out to be a priest whose handshake burns the tyro vampire's flesh, while her mother serves up a dish of sea trout braised in *garlic*. Sebastian eventually tucks into the family's pet white rabbit, leaving him wondering how to conceal the bloodstained remains in a pristine white bathroom. As the final touch, he looks into the bathroom mirror and sees his reflection fading away.

The vampirism in *Frostbiten* is a seemingly random mixture of science (it resembles rabies or drug addiction, and is spread by both the vaccine and biting) and superstition (garlic, mirrors). In *Near Dark* (a vampire film in which the word 'vampire' is never once used) Caleb's transformation into a vampire happens almost instantly after he has been nipped amorously on the neck by Mae; stumbling home across the fields as the sun rises, his skin starts to smoulder and burn. Like Sarah, he too is mistaken for a junkie.

Let the Right One In's version of becoming a vampire is sketched in with astonishing precision and economy when Virginia is bitten and infected. With her senses newly heightened, she finds everyday sounds exaggerated to an unbearable degree; the effect looks like the world's most debilitating hangover. Virginia is hypersensitive to light as well; her finger, touched by sunlight, starts to smoulder, and when she opens the blinds, the brightness is so painful she's immediately forced to close them again. The wound on her neck looks ugly and infected; in a fine bit of acting from Ika Nord, Virginia seems simultaneously drawn to and repelled by the bloodstained dressing. Desperate for blood, she goes outside and digs in the snow, round about where she and Lacke found the blood after Jocke's murder. Nord's every movement, every gesture indicates that what she is going through is excruciatingly painful and frightening. And we're aware that she's not the first to suffer these effects.

The morning after the bite: Virginia's finger, scorched by sunlight

'It's also done to show what Eli has gone through,' says Lindqvist. 'Eli has decided to live, whatever the cost.'

Virginia's problems with the transformation seem to be more to do with physical pain than with moral concerns; though she's drawn towards blood, it's never suggested she considers having to kill to obtain it. But the pain itself is more than enough for her. Strapped to a hospital bed, she says to Lacke: 'That kid, she must have infected me somehow. I don't want to live.' Turning into a vampire is a process so agonising she prefers suicide, and asks the nurse to open the blinds, knowing what the inevitable result will be.

The hospital:
Virginia bursts into
flame

THE VAMPIRE'S LIFESTYLE

ARE YOU, LIKE, POOR?

Traditional vampires live in large cobwebbed castles, or crumbling stately mansions. Dracula and his ilk sometimes dabble in real estate and, in *The Satanic Rites of Dracula* (1973) property development, but by and large, vampires are depicted as wealthy individuals who rarely have to worry about income or housing. It's assumed they have the financial nous to invest wealth, or the strength to steal it, or the time to amass it. (An interesting exception is Cora, the vampire heroine of Marc Behm's comic vampire novel *The Ice Maiden*, whose 'main problem was the rent. She owed the landlady fifteen hundred dollars. That was a disaster! Oh, Lord! If she were evicted, she'd really be in trouble. In fact, it would be fatal!')

Likewise, in *The Hunger*, centuries-old Miriam lives in a Manhattan brownstone (worth between $2.2million and $3.5million in today's market). In a welcome unexpected touch in the *Twilight* movies, the Cullen 'family' resides not in a castle or old dark house but an airy modern Frank Lloyd Wright-esque home. It's just as well that sunlight doesn't harm the Cullens, since the walls of their crib (reportedly owned in real life by a Nike executive) are lined with picture windows.

In *Let the Right One In*, on the other hand, Eli contents herself with a bog-standard flat on a Swedish housing estate, where her interest in decor stops at customising the bathroom to turn it into a light-tight nest. As with the rest of the flat, this 'customisation' looks hasty and improvised – covered windows and several layers of blankets. It's as though neither Eli nor Håkan expects to stay in one place for any length of time, but neither have they made provision for being constantly on the move – a set of lightweight, light-tight darkroom curtains, for example, which could be attached by strips of Velcro, or a zip-up light-tight vampire sleeping-bag. They seem to be living in the moment, without planning ahead, but without taking much pleasure from the moment either.

Eli and Håkan's flat bears all the hallmarks of an environment where the occupants have lost interest in the superficial trappings of life. Luxury, style and knowledge for knowledge's sake hold no joy for them. It's the opposite of Miriam's brownstone in

The Hunger, which is furnished with bourgeois taste and elegance. Eli's flat is furnished sparsely. It doesn't look comfortable at all. Håkan doesn't have a proper bed to sleep on; Eli sleeps in the bath, the nearest thing the flat can offer to a lightnight coffin. There are blankets, a lamp, a table and a box, and the floor clearly needs sweeping. 'It's very empty and dull and it stinks,' says Lindqvist. When Oskar sees Eli's flat for the first time, he asks her, 'Are you, like, poor?'

The vampire lifestyle: Eli's sparsely-furnished flat

But Eli is the opposite of 'poor'. 'See that egg there?' she says to Oskar, pointing to what looks like a Fabergé egg puzzle made of precious metal. 'If you sold it, you could buy a whole nuclear power plant.' It's a strange reference. Why a nuclear power plant? Is that the most expensive thing she can think of? On the table, alongside the egg, are: a troll with white hair, a doll, a lion, a toy rabbit, rings and a couple of small boxes. Are they toys people have given her, thinking she was a child? Or keepsakes she stole? Do they remind her of the human adolescence of which she herself was robbed? Or does each one represent someone befriended in her long existence, someone who first aroused her curiosity with the knick-knack the way Oskar did with the Rubik's Cube? And will the cube one day end up in this collection?

Since Eli has a Fabergé egg and a whole heap of jewellery at her disposal, it's clear the lack of furniture is not a lifestyle decision based on financial expediency, but the result of a lack of interest in her physical surroundings, almost certainly a consequence of having lived so long. We all like to think that, as vampires, we'd spend centuries learning foreign languages and a wide variety of musical instruments and, thanks to judicious investment, living it up in grand style in impeccably tasteful surroundings. (There's no rule that vampires should have impeccable taste, by the way. But it's always assumed they do.) But in truth, we'd probably just end up frittering the extra time away on the vampire version of Facebook or Twitter. Or we'd end up rootless nomads, like the bloodsuckers in *Near Dark*, never more than a couple of steps ahead of the cops or the FBI. Or we'd find ourselves trapped in a decaying suburb of Pittsburgh, stuck in a dead-end job, like *Martin*.

It's logical that bourgeois trappings would lose their allure after a couple of centuries, and surprising we don't see more vampires afflicted by the sort of been-there-done-that Weltschmerz endured by Emilia Marty, the 327-year-old heroine of Leoš Janáček's opera *The Makropulos Affair*, based on the play of the same name by Karel Čapek. Marty isn't a vampire, in that she doesn't need to drink blood to survive, but she has always behaved as she liked, with no thought of the consequences, and she expresses perfectly the psychological effect of a longevity when, in the final act of the opera, she rejects a chance to drink the potion that will enable her to live for another 300 years, and concludes:

What hideous solitude!
It's all in vain, Krista,
whether you sing or keep silent –
no pleasure in being good,
no pleasure in being bad.
No pleasure on earth,
no pleasure in heaven.
And one comes to learn
that the soul has died inside one.

Even in the essentially lighthearted *Cirque du Freak: The Vampire's Assistant* (2009), adapted from a series of children's novels by Darren Shan, Mr Crepsley the vampire (played affectingly by John C Reilly) replies to the young hero's assertion that 'Life isn't meaningless,' with the world-weary comment, 'Tell me that after 200 years of it, kid.'

But more than any film before it, *Let the Right One In* takes the vampire condition seriously and offers a 'realistic' view of the psychological consequences of longevity.

And what has Eli been doing all that time, apart from drinking blood? As we've seen with the Rubik's Cube, and as we will see later with the egg, she is fascinated by puzzles;

there's also a shot of her playing what looks like dominos on the floor of her flat. Anyone who has ever had a great deal of time to kill in an airport departure lounge can attest to the time-wasting properties of sudoku or crossword puzzles. When, in the near future, personal computers start becoming regular household items, Eli will no doubt discover computer games to be the ultimate eaters of time. Louis in *Interview with the Vampire* goes to the cinema (which enables him to see the sun rise for the first time in a century). Miriam and John in *The Hunger* play chamber music. When they're not fighting lycans, the vampires in *Underworld* appear to spend their time lolling around, looking decadent. But mostly, it seems, vampires have to organise their nightly schedule around the location and acquisition of sustenance, which of course they can't shop for in a supermarket; the nature of their lifestyle is dictated by the necessity to hunt and kill.

THE VAMPIRE'S NEMESIS

I'D LIKE TO TEAR THAT DAMNED KID LIMB FROM LIMB.

At the end of Hammer's *Dracula*, Dr Van Helsing (Peter Cushing) duly defeats Count Dracula by forcing him into a patch of sunlight, where, in an early, very basic example of the special effects which were to transform vampire movies in the 1980s, he crumbles into dust. The film was an enormous box-office success, leading to seven sequels (eight if one is to count the vampire-kung-fu hybrid, *The Legend of the Seven Golden Vampires* (1974)) and several non-Dracula vampire films.

Not all vampire movies of the 1960s followed the Hammer template of the Van Helsing-esque savant defeating evil. In Italy, Mario Bava's *Black Sunday* (1960) was a more oneiric version of the myth in which the sage doctor character, far from defeating the vampirelike witch, is instrumental in resuscitating her with his blood, and is subsequently himself turned into a vampiric demon, while the final segment of the same director's three-part portmanteau film *Black Sabbath* (1963) is an adaptation of Alexei Tolstoy's *The Family of the Vourdalak*, starring Boris Karloff as a patriarch who becomes a vampire and turns on his family.

In France, beginning with *Le viol du vampire* (1968), Jean Rollin directed a series of erotic vampire films in which there was scant opposition to his predominantly female, often lesbian vampires, and certainly no dusty old sages to threaten them with a good staking. And Roman Polanski subverted the Hammer formula with his Anglo-American horror-comedy *Dance of the Vampires/The Fearless Vampire Killers* (1967) which jokily acknowledges the existence of a gay vampire, and a Jewish vampire which sneers when threatened with a crucifix ('Oy vey, have you got the wrong vampire!'), and in which it's the self-regarding stupidity of the Van Helsing-like sage played by Jack MacGowran (a dead ringer for the evil doctor in *Vampyr*) which ultimately unleashes a plague of vampirism into the world – the very catastrophe he sought to avert.

The irreverent approach and ironic dénouement of *Dance of the Vampires* are more in tune with revisionist 1970s film-making than with the typical Hammer tale in which dark desires are defeated and the status quo restored; but the lush imagery – the innkeeper's daughter Sarah (Sharon Tate) importuned by a vampire while she's taking a bath, or the dance itself, with its human interlopers trying to blend into a roomful of rotting undead aristocracy – is hauntingly beautiful. As in *Let the Right One In*, snow plays an important part in the setting; Sarah, in her bathtub, first becomes aware of the vampire peering in through the skylight when snowflakes start falling around her; the characters travel around on sleighs and sledges, accompanied by the sounds of jingling harnesses and trotting hooves. The snow transforms the setting into a glittering landscape of fairytale and legend. It's logical, when you think about it, that vampires should gravitate towards the North, at least during the winter months when sunlight is scarce, an idea taken to its logical conclusion in *30 Days of Night* and *Frostbiten*. The fact that it never gets completely dark in northern climes in the summer, however, suggests that vampires could usefully migrate, like birds, towards the southern hemisphere, or even hibernate during the summer months. Pity the unwary traveller who finds himself on the aeroplane or ocean liner full of northern vampires headed south.

Filling the vampire-slayer's role in *Let the Right One In* is the unlikely figure of Lacke, but he's a long way from either Van Helsing or his young female successor, Buffy Summers. Lacke is intelligent but deadbeat, made cynical and casually cruel by years of disappointment, dulled by alcohol. He doesn't seem to have a job, instead preferring to spend his time drinking and grumbling. It's not clear whether he's ever really aware that he's dealing with a vampire as opposed to, say, a feral child, but since none of the adults in the film expresses out loud the possibility of a vampire at large, it's probably safe to say he isn't.

'Why would a kid kill Jocke?' Lacke, the unlikely vampire hunter

Lacke and Virginia appear to have a similar sort of relationship to that of Eli and Håkan, with Lacke, at least, taking his girlfriend for granted, until it's too late. 'I also see those two – Lacke and Virginia – as a reflection of Oskar and Eli if they should have stayed,' says Lindqvist, 'if they had taken the punches from the tormentors, if they had not chosen to be themselves, they would have turned into these two'. Lacke, though, would seem to have more in common with Håkan than with Oskar – both men are past their prime, addicts (one an alcoholic, the other addicted to Eli) pickled in self-pity and, unable to escape from the routine and dependencies in which they are trapped, fated to go through the motions of living rather than forge meaningful connections. Oskar, on the other hand, will eventually find himself with an opportunity to break out of the way of life which oppresses him.

The first indication we've had that Lacke might turn out to be Eli's chief antagonist is when he suddenly sits up in bed in the middle of the night and asks, as though he's been brooding over it, 'Why would a kid kill Jöcke?'. It doesn't occur to him to go to the police with his suspicions; perhaps, like Gösta (who decided not to tell the police about the murder he witnessed), he's afraid of being thought mad, or of coming under suspicion himself, or perhaps these men are survivors of the 1960s, with a lingering generational antipathy towards authority. Instead, Lacke says, 'I'd like to tear that damned kid limb from limb'.

Lacke's murderous rage towards Eli (who is, as far as he's aware, is still just a child) probably contains elements of guilt as well. He knows he didn't just fail to appreciate Virginia while she was still alive, he also rebuffed her cruelly in Gösta's flat, when he was mourning Jöcke's death in a remarkably selfish, unthinking manner. He seems to take a perverse pride in claiming that Jocke's death has hit him hardest out of everyone else present. 'Now that he's gone I have nothing left,' he moans, either forgetting or choosing to ignore that he is surrounded by friends and that his girlfriend is sitting right next to him. She looks hurt and tries to comfort him, but when he snaps at her impatiently ('You don't get it, you're so damn cold') she snatches up her coat and leaves, in tears. It's only when his other companions chide him that he follows her out, trying to catch up with her and offering, too late, to talk. She shakes her head sadly (actually, 'sadly' is too weak a term for the actress's expression, which conveys an entire adulthood of being psychologically abused and neglected, probably by this very same man), turns her back on him and climbs some badly lit steps leading to another part of the estate.

Lacke stays where he is, only moving when he hears a strange sound (it's the animal noise Eli makes when she drops from a tree on to Virginia's shoulders). Lacke hurries up the steps and sees Virginia on the ground, Eli crouched on top of her. Lacke shouts 'Get off her' and kicks Eli away. Seemingly stunned, Eli looks round, her mouth covered in blood, and for a moment it seems as if she's thinking of attacking Lacke as well. But then Gösta and another friend arrive on the scene, so she flees instead. (This is another indication that Eli doesn't particularly enjoy killing – judging by the vampire-to-victim ratio in the swimming-pool massacre, she could probably have taken on three drunks at once. Her decision to retire from the scene might also have something to do with a sudden attack of prudence – they are right in the middle of the housing estate, after all.)

Lacke, bent over the stricken Virginia, selfishly chooses this moment to say to her, 'I love you', but the only response he gets is a cry of pain; he's offering too little, too late. The next evening, when Virginia enters Gösta's flat, Lacke asks her where she's been and says he was worried about her, though one wonders why he didn't insist on spending the night with her after Eli's attack, when she would have been traumatised.

After Gôsta's cats attack Virginia and she falls downstairs, Lacke follows her to the hospital. Belatedly acknowledging what Virginia means to him, he sits next to her bed and talks about selling his father's postage stamp collection. One stamp is worth 80,000 kroner ('Then we'll buy that nice cottage'). He holds the stamp right in front of Ginia's face. She's strapped in, and doesn't react. He continues to talk about selling the stamps, planning their future together in a countryside idyll, though she's clearly not listening. And in the morning, she's dead.

'Everything's taken away from him by Eli,' says Lindqvist. 'You can thoroughly understand his hatred.'

As Lacke retraces his steps, his actions are cross-cut with those of Oskar. Lacke revisits the underpass where Jocke was killed. Meanwhile, Oskar has gone to Eli's apartment where he's sleeping on the ground wrapped in a blanket, like Håkan before him;. Eli has left him a note in her ornate handprinting: 'Hi, I'm in the bathroom. Please don't come in. Want to hang out tonight? I really like you. Yours, Eli.'

Lacke looks up at the covered window he saw at the start of the film. He seems at last to be making connections in his head. But instead of the viewer hoping he'll succeed in locating and destroying the killer, we have a feeling of mounting dread. Without bearing him any ill will (other than he was such a pig to Ginia while she was still alive) we don't want him to succeed; we're afraid for Eli, and for Oskar too.

The camera creeps through Eli's apartment to reveal Lacke, standing in the entrance hall. He walks through the flat and tears a corner of the paper away from the window, letting in light. He takes a knife from the kitchen. He doesn't notice Oskar under the table. Oskar has already made his choice between the world of his parents and that of Eli; before leaving for Eli's flat, he looked in on his sleeping mother, as if looking at her for the last time.

Lacke opens the bathroom door. The light doesn't work. Behind him, Oskar creeps out from beneath the table. In the bathroom, the camera switches to an overhead angle. Alfredson says: 'Hitchcock used this trick a lot in his films – to have a bird's eye angle before something violent happens, so it's a warning, sort of signal, to have the bird's eye point of view.' It's worth remembering that Hitchcock also used the overhead angle in *Psycho* – a film which, like *Let the Right One In*, hinges on gender ambiguity – to mask the killer's identity and prevent audiences spotting that the murderer of Detective Arbogast is not Mrs Bates, but Norman Bates dressed as his mother.

Lacke peels layers of blanket away from Eli, sleeping in the bathtub. Behind him, Oskar approaches the bathroom door. Eli looks peaceful as she sleeps, but the alert viewer can hear her stomach rumbling – a sign we already associate with her thirst for blood. Lacke holds the knife over Eli's neck. Oskar is creeping up behind him. Despite Lacke's desire for vengeance, he hesitates. Eli looks so young and vulnerable. Does he know she's a monster? Behind him, Oskar is standing in the bathroom doorway. He unsheaths his own knife. He has rehearsed this moment many times, but doesn't look so confident now he's confronting a real person instead of a tree. Lacke says to himself, 'I can't see a thing,' and yanks up a corner of the cardboard covering the window. Oskar lets out a cry of 'No!' which distracts Lacke momentarily, long enough for Eli to open her eyes. Lacke turns to face Oskar and throws down his own knife, apparently assuming that Oskar is no threat and ready to give up. With a growl, Eli leaps on Lacke's back and pulls him back into the bathroom. There are sounds of a struggle, Lacke grunting in pain and the sort of slooshy liquid noises we associate with Eli drinking blood. Oskar half-closes the door and retreats. Lacke's flailing hand leaves a streak of blood on the door jamb before it goes limp. There's the sound of a death rattle. Oskar, who now has his back to the bathroom door, is breathing heavily. He sheaths his knife and drops it. Eli, with blood around her mouth, comes up behind him, puts her arms around him and says, 'Thank you.'

It's a watershed moment for Oskar. While he hasn't killed for Eli, he has been instrumental in causing someone's death. It's an action, or an absence of action, which draws the two children together; from now on, they'll be looking out for each other. But our feelings are tinged with sadness. In a more traditional vampire movie, Lacke would be the hero, struggling to overcome his cynicism and dependence on alcohol to avenge his friend and his lover by standing up to the monster and ultimately defeating it. But all he does here is get himself killed, while our sympathies lie almost entirely with the monster and her human companion, so we are relieved when he doesn't succeed.

Nevertheless, we're left with a twinge of discomfort; for all Lacke's cynicism and drunken grumbling, he doesn't deserve to die. One of the underlying themes of the film is that life isn't fair; you don't always get what you deserve and good guys don't always win. But on the other hand, it's also a film in which it's not at all clear who the good guy *is*.

Eli's bathroom door, and the last of Lacke

THE VAMPIRE'S ASSISTANT

The vampire preys on the weak, so it's little wonder vampirism is often seen as a metaphor for capitalist exploitation. But reducing vampire movies to a single metaphor or allegory is like calling *Hamlet* a ghost story, or *À la recherche du temps perdu* a novel about homosexuality. The useful thing about movie monsters, but especially about vampires, is that they have always offered a multiplicity of metaphors, some of them overlapping, some purely subjective, and not all of them immediately obvious.

In *Let the Right One In*, as already discussed, the metaphors are even less obvious than usual, leaving the film's deeper meanings open to individual interpretation. Is it a love story between two outsiders? Is it the study of a serial-killer, or a rite-of-passage tale in which a boy learns to be true to his own nature, with a little help from a mysterious stranger? Or an imaginary friend yarn in which an alienated schoolboy summons a powerful supernatural predator to turn the tables on the bullies who have been tormenting him? Or is it simply the story of a vampire's assistant?

Just as Dr Frankenstein needs his hunchbacked Igor (or Fritz, or Otto) to rob graves, flick switches and sweep the floor of the laboratory, so the vampire needs his or her helpmate – perhaps even more than Dr Frankenstein, since a creature unable to tolerate sunlight but which nevertheless wants to live among humans inevitably has need of human assistance: to deal with bureaucracy and paperwork, to interact with estate agents during the daytime, to heft baggage, to get his or her hands dirty where the vampire loftily disdains such menial toil, to dispose of drained corpses or provide physical strength when the vampire is weakened by lack of sustenance, and to guard the sleeping vampire against his or her enemies during daylight hours, as does Oskar when Lacke finds Eli in the bathtub. Dracula manipulates and exploits Jonathan Harker and Renfield. Jerry Dandridge in *Fright Night* has Billy Cole to attend to his daytime needs. *Dance of the Vampires'* Count von Krolock has Koukol to do his heavy lifting.

Like all master-servant bonds, this one has echoes of the dominant-submissive power-playing of a sadomasochistic relationship, but though the vampire is dependant upon his assistant, he or she is always depicted as being the more powerful of the two – aristocrat and servant, villain and henchman, celebrity and PR manager, rock star and roadie. But it's a two-way street; the master is helpless without his servant, who will occasionally actively subvert the status quo to become the wielder of power, as we can see in films such as *The Servant* (1963) or, indeed, in PG Wodehouse's Bertie Wooster novels, in which Jeeves the valet holds the upper hand while pretending not to. It might be interesting to see a story in which the traditional vampire-servant dynamics are completely reversed - in which it's the helpmate who pulls the strings and the vampire who is the exploited victim (a set-up touched on in the first season of *True Blood* [2008–], in which vampire's blood is in demand as a drug, and a vampire is held captive by two addicts so they can use him as a supply). But although the vampire myth has its roots in the superstitions of peasants, it's the towering figure of Count Dracula which continues to shape our view of the vampire as an aristocrat who preys on the lower classes.

On one of its many levels, *Let the Right One In* relates a story we've rarely read or seen before – that of how someone becomes a vampire's assistant (though Darren Shan tackles it head-on in his young adult novel *Cirque du Freak* [2000] and its sequels, narrated by the young assistant). How did he come to meet the vampire? Did he become the vampire's lackey of his own free will, or was he coerced into it? Did he fall in love, as both Håkan and Oskar appear to have done, and to what degree was this love inspired by the vampire's supernatural magnetism? Or did he imagine a stint as a vampire's assistant would be a step on the road towards becoming a vampire himself and securing eternal life and youthfulness, as promised by Miriam in *The Hunger*?

In the novel, Håkan is a paedophile who has been fired from his job after 'someone who worked at the post office and who lived in the area had tipped off the other neighbours about what kind of mail, what kind of videos he received' (Lindqvist, 2007, p237). His home is firebombed by vigilantes and he becomes a suicidal alcoholic until, one day, Eli sits down next to him on a bench and says, 'You're going to stop drinking now. You are going to be with me. You are going to help me. I need you. And I'm going to help you' (ibid.). None of this is included in the film, where Håkan's past is left for the viewer to imagine. For all we know, Eli could have enrolled him while he was still young and cute, like Oskar, and has grown older and more desperate in her service, but nowadays, for an apparently young girl to be seen in the company of an older man who is not a close relative is enough to plant the suspicion of paedophilia in viewers' minds. But even without the back story, it's clear that Håkan is emotionally dependent on Eli, and senses that his position as her helpmate is under threat from her developing friendship with the boy next door.

In the novel, Håkan survives his fall from the hospital window, but as a zombie with a huge erect member and a sole remaining instinct, which is to physically consummate the relationship with Eli in the way he had never been able to in life. For obvious reasons, this wouldn't have worked on film. Or if it *had* worked, the results would have been an entirely different sort of movie – a knockabout hardcore porn horror-comedy, perhaps, more in the trashy B-movie tradition of Troma or Charles Band's Empire Pictures. It would certainly have clashed with the delicacy and elegance of Alfredson's vision.

To all appearances, the relationship between Oskar and Eli is an equal one, and their love is spiritual rather than sexual. But one of the most troubling aspects of the film is that the vampire-human bond is no more than a reflection of any inter-human relationship involving shifting degrees of dependency, emotional power struggles and the possibility that one party may (even unwittingly) be exploiting the other. In any psychologically 'healthy' relationship, the stronger party will resist the temptation to take advantage of the weaker, but the idea of no relationship being a truly equal partnership extends to the likelihood of one partner earning more money than the other, or dictating the other's behaviour, or threatening physical or psychological abuse, or ageing more rapidly, or sickening and dying before the other.

In our society, to be half of a couple is seen as an eminently desirable goal, one leading to marriage and children – the traditional family unit which is preceived as the rock on which society is based, hence the flourishing industry of dating services and the social rituals (parties, nightclubs, dating and so on) around which a large part of teenage and young adult life is based. Popular culture (music, films, novels, TV shows, fashion) preaches the desirability of the two-person unit so relentlessly one might almost suspect an organised conspiracy, but the picture it holds up only reflects what people want to believe – that no-one is truly alone in the world, that there is a perfect match for everyone, that they themselves are a desirable human being, attractive and important enough to occupy someone's thoughts. In short, that they have worth, and their lives have meaning. The romantic couple is often seen as two halves of a whole, linked by love, while the single man or woman is to be pitied as unloved, barren, eccentric, an outsider.

In real life, romantic passion invariably develops into a less intense but more pragmatic partnership based as much if not more on financial expediency, physical compatability or social convenience. And the initial attraction which draws two people together is rarely as pure and spiritual as romantic love's apologists would have you believe, nor is it simply 'chemistry'; it's a combination of a wide range of factors, both positive and negative, of which we may only be subconsciously aware. We may be drawn to the other person because we have experiences in common, or because they remind us of a parent, celebrity or ex-lover, someone important in our lives or dreams. Or because they represent the lives we think we want to lead, or we believe association with them will boost our social standing, or advance our careers, or offer financial stability or incite admiration and envy from our peers. Or we may be drawn to them because they represent to us the elements lacking from our own lives. Or perhaps simply because they're good company.

The relationship between Oskar and Eli appears to be innocent (or as innocent as any relationship can be when one of the parties is a supernatural serial killer), yet – like most relationships – it is founded on expediency and association. Oskar and Eli and very obviously two halves of a whole: male and (apparently) female, yin and yang, light and dark, old and young. At the same time, they have a lot in common – they both look young, both look the same age, both are outsiders and loners, and they're both victims who have been forced into aggression by cruelty and persecution. For Eli, Oskar represents the childhood that was stolen from her, as well as companionship in a long and lonely existence, and, perhaps, the support of a human being who is younger, prettier and more fun than Håkan. And for Oskar, Eli is a fellow outcast who doesn't just represent the companionship he has never had, but who understands his loneliness and murderous urges without judging him. But the film also shows the positive aspects of a close friendship in the way both individuals can unite against the rest of the world, drawing encouragement and support from one another.

VAMPIRE RULES

YOU HAVE TO INVITE ME IN.

The public fascination with vampires is surely due, in part, to the panoply of rules and rituals which have arisen around them. They drink blood. They cast no reflection. They can turn into bats, or wolves, or other creatures. They are capable of hypnotising their victims. They can be destroyed by a stake through the heart, decapitation, fire, running water, sunlight. They are allergic to crucifixes, holy water and garlic. And they are unable to cross a threshold unless invited. Vampire films and novels often ring changes on these rules, but they all pay lip-service to some or all of them to some degree.

Eli is not dead, though she drinks blood to survive and must avoid sunlight, but both these characteristics could be explained by a non-supernatural medical condition, such as porphyria. The only other rule to which she seems susceptible is that of needing an invitation to cross a threshold, the rule which gives the film (and the novel before it) its title. One of the key scenes in *Let the Right One In* is when Oskar asks Eli what would happen if she came into his flat without an invitation, and she proceeds to show him. 'From the horror genre perspective, I know this is quite an original scene,' says Linqvist. 'You've never seen what actually happens.'

In Goethe's *Faust*, Mephistopheles is at first unable to come and go as he pleases – he needs an invitation, just as man has to allow the Devil and temptation into his life. Mephistopheles first appears to Faust in the form of a black poodle, which Faust must first invite into his abode; he also needs permission to leave. Faust grants it willingly. Mephistopheles tells Faust: 'It is a law of ghosts and devils too.'

The vampire's need for an invitation, however, seems to be an invention of Stoker. In Chapter XVIII of *Dracula*, when Van Helsing is listing the rules governing the vampire, he says:

> He cannot go where he lists; he who is not of nature has yet to obey some of nature's laws – why we know not. He may not enter anywhere at the first, unless there be someone of the household who bid him to come; though afterwards he can come as he please. (Stoker, 1897/Penguin 1979, p287).

We see this in action in films such as Hammer's *Dracula*, where Lucy welcomes Dracula by flinging open the French windows of her room, removing her crucifix and generally behaving like a woman expecting the arrival of her demon lover at any second. It's relayed more obviously in, for example, *The Lost Boys*, where the head vampire says, 'Don't ever invite a vampire into your house, you silly boy. It renders you powerless'.

In Tobe Hooper's telefilm of *Salem's Lot* (1979), adapted from Stephen King's novel, Danny Glick sees his dead younger brother Ralphie hovering outside his bedroom window, but must open the window to let him in. The next day Danny collapses and is taken to hospital where he again opens the window for Ralphie, this time with fatal consequences. The following night, vampire Danny appears in his turn, hovering at the window of his erstwhile friend Mark Petrie, scratching at the glass and urging him to, 'Open the window, Mark. Please. Let me in. It's OK, Mark, I'm your friend'. But Mark is a horror fan, and though he seems half-hypnotised, he manages to repel the dead boy with a crucifix plucked from the base of one of the monster figurines he collects.

Elsewhere in the same film Mike Ryerson, who has died in Jason Burke's guest bedroom, returns to the house as a vampire, prompting Jason to say, 'Get out, I revoke my invitation', which, combined with a brandished crucifix, is enough to drive the vampire backwards through the window. In *True Blood* after an argument with her vampire boyfriend Bill, human waitress Sookie says to him, 'I rescind your invitation', before walking him backwards through her house to the door. In the second season of TV series *Buffy the Vampire Slayer*, a major plot thread involves Buffy trying to find a way of reversing her invitation to her vampire boyfriend Angel after he turns evil.

Most vampire films simply show vampires being physically unable to enter dwellings into which they haven't been invited. We've always assumed there's an invisible or perhaps psychic barrier which keeps them out. We've seen one or two vampires (Angel, for example) stopping abruptly as though they've encountered a glass door, but we've never actually seen them struggling against this strict door policy or exploring its limits; perhaps the results would be like Marcel Marceau encountering an invisible wall.

Let the Right One In is the first film to propose that vampires may be physically capable of entering a building or flat without an invitation, but avoid doing so because the results are so messy, painful and possibly hazardous to their health. So when Eli rings Oskar's doorbell, and she says, 'You have to invite me in,' and he teasingly asks the question that may have occurred to us, 'What happens if I don't?' she shows him. He beckons her in, thinking it's all a joke and watching half-curious, half-sceptical. She starts breathing more heavily, like someone in pain, and her innards start making strange noises, as though they're rearranging themselves. As Oskar looks on, fascinated but horrified, a splodge of blood soaks through the back of her shirt. Blood seeps out from around the roots of her hair, from her ears and eyes, at which point Oskar can stand it no longer and darts forward, yelling, 'No! You can come in!'

'You have to invite me in.' Eli shows Oskar what happens when he doesn't

It's an alarming effect, with few precedents. In Martin Campbell's film version of *Casino Royale* (2006), James Bond's adversary Le Chiffre suffers from a medical condition known as haemolacria, which causes him to weep tears of blood. This is as nothing next to Brian De Palma's *The Fury* (1978) in which a tormented psychic uses his paranormal powers to exsanguinate his doctor while she is spinning in the air. Medical thrillers such as *Outbreak* (1995) sometimes feature ebola-like viruses which cause severe bleeding.

This is the only time in the film we see evidence of Eli's supernatural nature with our own eyes. True, we see her scaling the wall of the hospital, but not in close-up; for all we know, she could be a talented free-climber. She tells Oskar she flew through his bedroom window, but we don't see her actually doing it. We see her attacking and killing people, but it doesn't take supernatural powers to do that, even if she does seem to be unusually strong for a child. Even in the swimming-pool massacre, we don't actually see her killing Conny, Jimmy and Martin; she could be a gifted martial arts expert. But when she starts to bleed from her pores, it offers incontrovertible proof that the film is about the love between a human boy and a girl who is not human at all. However, when

Oskar asks her, 'Who are you?' Eli replies, 'I'm like you'. (She is, in fact, more like Oskar than he or we can guess at this stage, being of the same gender.) And she is indeed a lot like him, as she reminds him by quoting the first words she heard him say: 'So scream, squeal!'

Oskar protests, 'I don't kill people'. To which Eli responds, 'No, but you'd like to if you could. Right? I do it because I have to'.

Though Eli doesn't hypnotise her victims, she does seem capable of a sort of Vulcan Mind Meld-type telepathy, when she says to Oskar, 'Be me, for a little while'. It's here in the novel that we get the flashbacks filling in her history and origins as a prepubescent boy who was castrated, but the film skips these, though once again we get a glimpse of Eli's 'old' face.

Oskar, peeking through the door as Eli gets dressed after cleaning herself up, has a fleeting glimpse of a scar on her pubic area. It could be clumsy scarring from an appendectomy, or an ovarectomy, but, as explained in Lindqvist's novel (p388–391), it's a penectomy. Since this takes place after the mind-meld, perhaps Oskar is already aware of what it represents.

*****

On a technical level, the weakest scene in *Let the Right One In* is the one in which Virginia is attacked by cats in Gösta's flat. Earlier, we have seen a cat hissing at Eli through a shop window. But some of the creatures in Gösta's flat look too obviously computer-simulated, and the results verge on slapstick, especially a shot from the balcony where Gösta has cravenly taken refuge while Virginia flails around in the background, trying to shake off the cats that are biting her. Virginia makes a dash for the stairs with cats still clinging to her like a mangy fur coat, and falls down the steps; there's an immediate cut to the hospital, where she's still flailing around while being wheeled along on a stretcher, with Lacke following behind.

The cats' violent reaction to the vampires suggests a sensitivity to another animal or predator in the vicinity; they react with hissing and flattened ears, the way they might react to a dog or another, more powerful cat. And indeed Eli makes an animal noise as she launches her attacks, and, while she lies in wait up a tree, makes a strange noise which might almost be a sort of purring. The way she laps up blood from the floor is also reminiscent of the actions of a cat.

The cat attack on Virginia is not the first film in which animals are shown as being sensitive to the presence of monsters. The shapeshifters in *Sleepwalkers* (1992), from a screenplay by Stephen King, are opposed by neighbourhood cats, which besiege the house where the shapeshifters are staying. King evidently thinks of cats as the good guys, since in the final story of *Cat's Eye* (1985), a portmanteau collection of three adaptations of King stories, the cat heroically saves little Drew Barrymore from a breath-stealing troll. But it's not just cats. In *Near Dark*, Caleb's horse reacts to Mae, who says, 'Horses don't like me'. In *The Lost Boys*, the young hero's Alaskan Malamute, Nanook, attacks the vampire intruders, while in *Bram Stoker's Dracula*, the animals in the zoo react with wild noises and panicked behaviour to Dracula's approach.

The animals are reacting, one imagines, to the presence of a creature they sense contravenes the laws of nature. Animals often predict natural disasters, such as earthquakes; they seem to know when the world is out of joint or when the natural order is disturbed. And vampires, the walking dead, are not natural but *supernatural*.

THE VAMPIRE'S DEPARTURE

I'VE GOT TO GO AWAY.

Traditional vampire films can have only one ending: the vampire is destroyed, either by being staked through the heart, decapitated, exposed to daylight or burned. *Let the Right One In*, as everyone will have realised by now, is not a traditional vampire film.

The ending can be interpreted in several different ways, some of these interpretations being sillier than others :

1. Eli saves Oskar, they simply live happily ever after, and we're not supposed to wonder about what happens after the end of the film.

2. Eli saves Oskar, and they go off to find another town, where he will learn to kill to provide her with blood. But, like Håkan before him, he will grow old and ugly, and eventually she will discard him and replace him with a younger model. Lindqvist has written (and is reportedly revising) an epilogue to *Let the Right One In* in the form of a short story called *Let the Old Dreams Die*, specifically to counter this cynical interpretation of the ending. In the new story (so far published only in embryonic form in a Swedish publication) Eli turns Oskar into a vampire, which brings us to...

3. Eli saves Oskar, and will later turn him into a vampire so they can be companions for ever. In which case, they will still need to find a human helper, as it will be difficult for two vampire children to survive on their own without attracting the attention of social services.

4. Eli doesn't save Oskar. She left in a taxi and doesn't come back. The ending in which she attacks the bullies and saves him is a wish fulfilment death-dream as he's drowning, a narrative device originating, probably, in Ambrose Bierce's story *An Occurrence at Owl Creek Ridge* (1891) and recurring in plenty of horror films, such as *Carnival of Souls* (1962) and *Jacob's Ladder* (1990).

5. There never was any Eli to begin with. The ending in which she saves him from the bullies is, again, a wish fulfilment death-dream, and he drowns, dreaming as he does so that his imaginary friend arrives in the nick of time to rescue him.

6. Eli saves Oskar and they set up house in another town, where Eli is trapped and

destroyed by vampire-hunters and Oskar is sentenced to six years in a juvenile correctional facility.

The film, in fact, has three endings, two of them false. After the death of Lacke and the reaction from neighbours who have apparently been disturbed by the noise (though Eli kills Lacke during daylight hours, so one can't help feeling they're being a little fussy) Eli tells Oskar, 'I've got to go away'. They kiss, leaving Oskar with blood on his mouth; to use a hunting term, he has been 'blooded'. They have shared culpability for the death of Lacke. But just as it seems his relationship with Eli is signed, sealed and delivered, Oskar will find himself on his own again.

The first false ending has no dialogue, just the poignant music accompanying a montage, scored and edited in such a way that it *seems* final, even if it's not. The montage consists of: Oskar's mother upset at him (presumably because he disappeared for a day without telling her where he was going); Oskar closing the door of his bedroom against her; Oskar straightening his toy cars; Oskar reading the newspaper report headlined, 'WHO KILLED THE MAN IN THE ICE?'; a taxi driving away from the building in the night; Oskar glimpsed through the window, looking abandoned; the deserted front of the building; Oskar walking through Eli's deserted flat; Oskar, in his underpants, gazing sadly out of his bedroom window, placing his palm against the glass as he did at the beginning of the film, his reflection once again blurred. As he pulls his hand away, the palm-print fades from the glass, as though he never really existed.

For a few days, Oskar had a friend, but he's alone again. Nothing much has changed, except that, for a short while, he has known happiness and companionship, so now he's even sadder than before. This is the Sad Ending. As in many of the films of Roman Polanski (including *Dance of the Vampires*, *Chinatown* [1974], *The Tenant* [1976], *Pirates* [1986], *Frantic* [1988]) the protagonist has come full circle and ended up more or less where he started, sadder but none the wiser for his experiences. Life is a vicious circle; nothing ever gets better; everyone repeatedly makes the same mistakes. Oskar is exactly where we first met him – trapped behind the glass of his bedroom window, looking out on the world. The bullies have been temporarily bested, but he is even more hopelessly alone than before. The film could end there, though it would undoubtedly leave us feeling melancholy. The street is empty, the jungle gym deserted.

But wait! There's more to come. The second ending begins with Oskar once again gazing sadly out of the window – this time in daylight. He's weeping softly to himself, until the phone rings and he answers it. It's Martin, saying, 'Mr Avila wanted to know if you're coming tonight'. Oskar wants to know why; Martin gives an unsatisfactory answer before saying, 'It was good, by the way, what you did to Conny. He had it coming'. Perhaps Oskar has made a friend after all. Eli was just the practice he needed to enable him to interact with his classmates. But no; Martin is calling from a pay-phone, with Conny, his elder brother Jimmy and Andreas sniggering behind him. It's a trap, and Oskar walks straight into it.

The following scenes are choreographed very precisely. In the changing rooms, the camera creeps around a corner to show Oskar putting on his plimsolls, though he is almost immediately accosted by Mr Avila, who proposes aqua aerobics. All the camera movements are slow and ominous and creeping, which together with the sound of running water, the echoing locker-room and corridors, stokes feelings of mounting dread in the spectator. We are aware that something terrible is about to happen, and we fear Oskar won't be able to cope with it now he's on his own.

Martin appears, loitering as though waiting for a prearranged signal. A door opens. There's a close-up of someone pouring accelerant over something in the dark.

The putting on of the plimsolls was obviously a redundant exercise, since when we next see Oskar, he's in the water, exercising joyfully to the sound of 'Flash in the Night' issuing from a transistor radio by the pool's edge. Mr Avila is urging him on, marching on the spot. The camera approaches him from the point of view of Martin; we see their legs and feet – with Oskar in the water behind them – as Martin goes up on tiptoe to say something to Mr Avila, who reacts with 'What? Christ!' and dashes away, pausing only to scoop up his keys.

Outside, in the snow, the contents of a skip are ablaze. Mr Avila walks briskly out and shouts, 'Call the fire department! Fire!' Jimmy watches him go. Martin, meanwhile, has taken Mr Avila's place, marching on the spot. Oskar looks up at him delightedly, smiling wide enough to break our hearts, as we know something terrible is about to happen. Martin gives a sadistic little smirk, seeming to enjoy having lured Oskar into the trap, and glances over towards the entrance to the pool.

The following occurs in a single take: Martin stops marching as Jimmy, Conny and Andreas enter in the background and start making their way along the length of the pool; Jimmy says 'Beat it!' to the other kids (all of them smaller) who scramble out of the pool and run out of the hall; Jimmy approaches the camera until his chest is in medium close-up, whereupon he flicks upen a knife; the camera moves up to include his head in the frame as he saunters along the edge of the pool and takes off his jacket; beside him, Andreas and Conny exchange glances; the camera pans round to show Oskar alone in the pool, dwarfed by Jimmy, who's crouching down in the foreground; Jimmy asks, 'Do you know who I am?'

At the swimming-pool: Conny's older brother Jimmy takes charge

We don't really know who Jimmy is, other than he's Conny's older brother, but we're pretty sure we don't want to know; he's about sixteen or seventeen, with a bad complexion and a weak but shifty look. Jimmy explains the rules of what he calls, 'a little contest'. If Oskar can stay underwater for three minutes, he'll just get nicked. But if he can't, Jimmy will poke one of his eyes out. 'An eye for an ear, right?' Clearly, Jimmy is a horrible sadist, and maybe the reason Conny feels the need to pick on someone weaker than himself; in a previous scene, we've already seen Jimmy teasing his younger brother for being deaf in one ear, suggesting he habitually preys on anyone who is weak and defenceless and that Conny compensates by dealing out misery to other, weaker boys. Jimmy is the least sympathetic character in the film; if the film ended with the death of Lacke, we would feel ambivalent; but we can't wait for Jimmy to get his come-uppance.

Oskar says, 'But that's impossible', to which Jimmy replies, 'That's your problem'. Conny kicks the radio into the water, which stops the music abruptly. Jimmy beckons to Oskar, who approaches him resignedly, presumably thinking he may as well get it over with.

Jimmy grabs him by the hair and pushes him under the water.

Oskar underwater

The editing here is rapid by the standards of much of the film, and makes it seem as though the young actor playing Oskar really is having to hold his breath for a long time. But the shots of him beneath the surface, with Jimmy still clutching his hair, are interspersed with the reactions of the others, making the underwater shots seem more protracted and agonising than they really are. Conny starts to look less smug, Martin bites his lip nervously and Andreas, the smallest and most reluctant of the bullies (and the one who wept while hitting Oskar), looks uncomfortable, glances at Conny and then up at the clock, where the second hand is shown in big close-up. There's a sense that the younger boys now realise events are spiralling out of their control, that Jimmy is taking things too far. Andreas goes and sits down, distancing himself from what's happening, and puts his head in his hands. It's this action that will save his life.

While we are in the pool with Oskar, outside noises are muffled by the water. But there's another sound in the distance; it might be a door or window slamming, or being smashed. We can also hear Oskar whimpering and letting out bubbles. He raises an arm; he's in distress now, so obviously that Conny protests to his brother, saying, 'Jimmy...'. Jimmy yells at him to shut up, and yells it again when Martin says, 'Let's go, Conny'. Neither boy moves. Jimmy looks round as though he's heard something. Or maybe he's just having second thoughts. If so, it's too late.

During the following sequence, we remain underwater with Oskar, though since his eyes are closed he doesn't see what we see. The sounds are muffled by the water. There's a loud crash, followed by the noise of breaking glass and a sort of distant animal howling, or perhaps it's screaming. Something flashes past in the water in the foreground, so fast we can't focus on it, but it could be Martin, because the next moment we see his legs kicking as he's hauled back across the surface of the pool; the legs go limp before they're suddenly yanked upwards. Still in the background, a severed head falls into the pool and floats gently to the bottom, leaking blood. There's a wet tearing sound and Jimmy's hand yanks at Oskar's hair, then slackens its grip before we see his severed arm float past. Almost immediately, another arm enters the pool, the bloodstained hand grasping Oskar and hauling him up out of the water.

Oskar surfaces, gasping and looking dazed but otherwise unharmed, and opens his eyes. We see what he sees, which is an out of focus extreme close-up of Eli's green eyes, filling the frame. (As Kim Newman writes, 'It's rarely noticed outside of Sergio Leone that widescreen is the perfect frame for eyes.' [*Sight & Sound*, May 2009, p69]). There are a few spots of blood and some strands of damp hair across her face. The eyes come into clear focus. They gaze intently. Oskar, gazing back at her, breaks out in a radiant smile. Though Eli's eyes are still all we can see of her face, it's clear she's smiling back at him.

Rescuer and rescued: Eli's eyes, Oskar's smile

The sequence ends with a wide shot of the pool. Oskar and Eli are nowhere to be seen, but Martin's corpse lays sprawled at the water's edge in the background. Jimmy and Conny lie dead nearer the camera. It's unclear who has lost his head, but it seems to be Jimmy, who's lying in the biggest pool of blood. Andreas is still sitting to one side, head in hands and sobbing quietly to himself.

Fade to black. Music.

This is the Second False Ending. The film could end here, leaving us more or less satisfied since the bullies have got their come-uppance – though perhaps feeling a little uncomfortable too, since even bullying, however nasty, isn't a capital offence. It's hard to feel sorry for Jimmy, whose behaviour bordered on the psychopathic and who really did seem prepared to let Oskar drown; but though we dislike Conny and Martin, did they really deserve to die? No matter, Eli doled out rough justice and rescued her friend, just as we'd hoped she would.

On first viewing, for a few horrible moments while Oskar was still underwater, I thought the film-makers were going to play the deathdream card, by having him imagine a rescue which never came. I'm glad they didn't. But it doesn't end there. Not quite.

Snow is falling across the black screen, just as it did at the start of the film.

The camera creeps slowly around the seatback in a seemingly deserted railway carriage to show Oskar, sitting on his own by the window as snow-covered countryside flashes past. He's not on his own, though, not this time. There's a knocking from a large trunk on the floor next to him. Oskar responds by tapping out the Morse code for 'kiss'.

This is the Real Ending of Let the Right One In. And in a way, it's a new beginning as well. We leave Oskar and Eli on their way to a new life.

It's a classic 'happy ending' in that we leave them at what is probably the optimum point in their story: young, in love with each other, and free. Each has saved the other's life, they trust each other completely and from now on they can be together.

We're not supposed to think too hard about the trail of corpses they leave behind them. Of course, Oskar's mother will report her son's disappearance to the police. The school will come under attack for the violence perpetrated on its premises; there will be an inquiry, and Mr Avila will probably be disgraced and lose his job. The press will have a field day. Lacke's corpse is presumably still in Eli's old flat; soon it will be discovered, and detectives will link the flat to Håkan. Perhaps they will also link it to the strange and inexplicable death of Virginia. Perhaps they will conclude that Oskar has been abducted by a paedophile ring to which Håkan belonged. Or perhaps they will dig around in Håkan's past and find evidence that his 12-year-old 'daughter' isn't all she appears to be.

And when Oskar and Eli arrive at their destination, wherever that may be, what then? How will two 12-year-olds, one of whom is unable to go out during the day, be able rent a flat? Will they be obliged to 'befriend' an adult? Will social services come a-knocking, and ask why they're not in school? How will a small boy with looks as distinctive as Oskar's be able to come and go without attracting unwanted attention from the authorities, or even neighbours who may have seen a photograph of him on the news – for his mother, surely, will have provided the police with a picture, and it will be broadcast all over the media? How will Eli keep herself supplied in blood without arousing suspicion? How will Oskar find enough to eat?

But then *Let the Right One In* is the rare sort of horror film that goes on giving, long after the final credits have rolled. And it's not just a horror film but also a love story and a romantic fantasy, but a romantic fantasy grounded firmly in everyday reality. And that's one of the most miraculous achievements of the film – that it is in itself yin and yang, light and dark, male and female, romantic and realist – an amalgam of opposites which come together in one perfect whole, like Oskar and Eli.

Oskar and Eli on their way to a new life

Printed and bound by CPI Group (UK) Ltd, Croydon, CR0 4YY

13/04/2025

14656604-0003